M000235424

NEW DAD
BABY HACKS

A Contemporary Guide for Dads
Strategies for the 1st Year That
every First time Father Needs

By William Harding

© Copyright _____ 2022 - All rights reserved
William Harding.

The content contained within this book may not be reproduced, duplicated, or transmitted without direct written permission from the author or the publisher.

Under no circumstances will any blame or legal responsibility be held against the publisher, or author, for any damages, reparation, or monetary loss due to the information contained within this book. Either directly or indirectly. You are responsible for your own choices, actions, and results.

Legal Notice:

This book is copyright protected. This book is only for personal use. You cannot amend, distribute, sell, use, quote or paraphrase any part, or the content within this book, without the consent of the author or publisher.

Disclaimer Notice:

Please note the information contained within this document is for educational and entertainment purposes only. All effort has been executed to present accurate, up to date, and reliable, complete information. No warranties of any kind are declared or implied. Readers acknowledge that the author is not engaging in the rendering of legal, financial, medical or professional advice. The content within this book has been derived from various sources. Please consult a licensed professional before attempting any techniques outlined in this book.

By reading this document, the reader agrees that under no circumstances is the author responsible for any losses, direct or indirect, which are incurred as a result of the use of the information contained within this document, including, but not limited to, — errors, omissions, or inaccuracies.

Just For you!

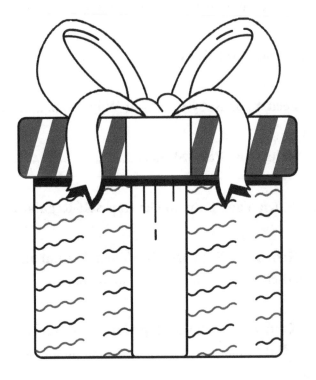

A FREE GIFT TO OUR READERS

10 Step **Action** plan that you can download now. Feel confident and prepared for your new born right now!

http://williamhardingauthor.com/

Table of Contents

Introduction

"Any man can be a father, but it takes someone special to be a dad." – Anne Geddes.

A nurse in scrubs just handed you a bundle, and holding it feels foreign. It is a bit of a wriggly thing and seems uncomfortable, like a butterfly emerging from a cocoon. It seems like a doll that little children play with for a moment, but this one has life-like skin. It looks a little other-worldly and a bit alien. You are unsure if you are looking at reality or a vision brought about by sleeplessness. The nurse congratulates you on being a new father from the other end of your tunnel vision.

You suddenly feel like you are juggling eggs and nearly drop the bundle. Your head pops as if waking up when nodding off at the wheel of a car. This is a newborn, and the little bundle is yours. It is what you spent the last nine months changing your life for so that you could safely get here, to this moment, holding the brand new life you created with your partner. As if on cue, it starts to cry. Or it may have been crying the whole time, and you are just beginning to hear it. You know you are already doing something wrong and your experience as a father has barely even started.

This baby is pretty complicated. It has moving parts you can't control and is powered by some artificial intelligence. There aren't any buttons or knobs to make it easy to operate. It isn't like the camera you just bought to document your experience of fatherhood. Immediately, you want to look for the owner's manual. You think to ask the nurse a question, but she seems busy with other important things right now. Besides that, you have no idea what to ask.

You feel about as comfortable as if someone handed you a live salmon. A crying salmon. What would you do with a salmon? Hand it to your partner. She'll know what to do. She always knows what to do with things like this.

-----

*As helpless as that sounds, that's what it could be like if you go into fatherhood blindly. Every cry and whimper will just be telling you that you've made yet another mistake. Within no time, you'll want to do everything you can to keep from touching the baby, so you don't set off its alarms. All it will ever tell you is that you are doing something wrong, and you want to avoid the consequence of the rejection. It will stay that way until you learn what is really happening.

* Here's the truth. What seems to be the interminable announcement of your failure is just a baby crying because that is part of the way they communicate before they learn to talk. Any avoidance you practice will make the baby sense you don't want to be there. You have to get in and take your lumps and snubs for a little bit until you get used to the baby and it gets used to you. The crying will just keep happening, but at least you can tell that your effort and wait were successful.

*The hard truth is that children do not come with a manual, but they do have built-in mechanisms designed to make you pay attention.

What they are saying as they cry and wriggle is a natural and innate way of communicating what are, for now, their basic needs and discomforts. These pages are here to help you make sense of the new language and prepare you for all the nuances of taking the helm as a dad.

This book is your owner's manual for the first year of your baby's life. It provides a holistic view, not just the simple nuts and bolts of the baby but also what will likely happen to you, your partner, your relationship, your environment and the world around you. You'll discover a plethora of tips just as you'd expect from any owner's manual, such as:

- How to baby-proof your home
- The real reasons why your baby cries
- Working with the baby's feeding schedule
- Problems that keep your baby awake
- Soothing and bonding with your infant
- What to feed your baby and what to avoid
- Keeping the relationship with your partner strong
- Exercising your baby's mental and emotional health

No matter how you have prepared for this part of your life, you will be surprised and likely amazed at the experience itself because it is anything but predictable. A whirling dervish entered onto your stage and will deliver a performance — part angel, part chaos. Even with the best preparation, you are guaranteed to experience something distinctly new and perhaps be surprised by fresh emotions. The sooner you come to terms with the chaos and rush of new emotions, the sooner you experience the joy of your little angel. Or something like that.

This first year will help you set the tone for a life-long relationship with this unique, new, unpredictable being. You can't expect to mold or itemize what is to come with any certainty, which is part of the delight. The one guarantee is that this will be an experience like no other. You hold the ticket for the trip of a lifetime, and it is time to find out what to expect along the way.

One thing you can never really know before it happens is how you will be as a father. Everyone handles the stresses, joys and changes differently. Knowing what's to come gives you a leg up on the situation. The thing you need to do first is survive the 24 hours after the baby is born.

Chapter 1

Surviving the First 24 Hours After Birth

The first few hours after your child's birth will be pretty intense, no matter how well it goes and how prepared you think you are. The first 24 hours are not so much critical but more a matter of adapting to the nuance and reality of being a dad.

Right at the moment of birth, you should have already made decisions about "catching the baby" (where you actually step in to have a literal hand in the delivery) and cutting the umbilical cord. You really can't have a weak stomach to do this or be prone to fainting. The doctor will assist you to be sure you don't do anything wrong. But you can not wait until the last minute to decide. Remember, you can always change your mind about stepping away from hands-on involvement if you start feeling wobbly in the knees. I do not get queasy and never passed out, but I was afraid of making a mistake.

You will mostly notice a bit of a mess in the first few moments after the birth. The baby will come out squashed, mottled and coated with vernix — a substance that has helped shield the baby's skin in utero. The goop and goo might be a little overwhelming if you don't know what is coming. I distinctly remember the afterbirth plopping out as if my partner couldn't stop herself from ejecting her organs with the child, as if the dam had broken. Even when you know that is coming, that's a moment even your partner will never see and to be honest, I am not sure I am happy I did.

It is worth noting that some cultures promote eating the (placenta). It is a rather unique, temporary organ — just there to serve its purpose during pregnancy. It is also something that has cultural meaning for some groups. It is used in traditional Chinese medicine and is commonly ingested by many species of animals. While I am an adventurous eater, this was beyond my personal scope of culinary interest, and no doctor ever suggested it. The act has gotten press in recent years as a celebrity fad and may be more popular with alternative birthing styles (e.g., people who choose to do water-birthing or those who use midwives). There are claims that the organ contains a mixture of nutrients and hormones that can help the mother recover from birth more quickly. But as many resources say, any benefits are offset by toxins that the organ stores and can pose food safety concerns. Some believe that any benefits are psychosomatic. Medical advice is outside this book's scope; therefore, it is up to you to do the research to see if the option interests you.

Your baby may be a little blue initially, and the wailing cries you expect may not be immediate. When the baby starts to breathe their first breaths, the color will shift to an expected shade. Remain calm, trust in the expertise of the people there to do the job, and breathe deeply. During the birth of our firstborn, the umbilical cord had wrapped around the baby's neck and she came out blue and not breathing. As the nurse carried the baby to the incubator cart, it seemed limp and lifeless to me and a deep panic set in because all I saw was a stillbirth. That was one thing none of the prep classes and materials I came across ever mentioned as a possibility. The nurse maintained calm as she went about her business, wiping things down to clean up, rubbing the baby's feet, and repeatedly glancing at the clock. I could not even look at my wife because I wasn't about to let on about my panic.

I felt the urge to jump in and whack the baby's behind like you may have seen on TV, in movies or in videos. My cooler head prevailed as I knew I had to trust the experts; there was no way I knew more than them. The first cry burst out a moment later, the child became animated, and her color changed almost immediately. Little did I know that motion would begin a cascade that would be difficult to quell. Until school began, that girl wouldn't stop moving all day until after she was asleep. One thing to take from my experience is to realize that the doctors know more than you do. They will generally let you know if there is cause for concern, like they let me know about the twisted umbilical cord.

A few tests take place almost immediately. The nurse will measure and weigh the child as they go about their routine. They take an APGAR score within the first minute of the birth to measure the relative health status of the baby. They continue to take APGAR measurements if the score remains below seven. See the "APGAR Scores" sidebar for more information about the test.

APGAR Scores

APGAR stands for Appearance, Pulse, Grimace, Activity, and Respiration. The scores are a means of quickly evaluating a baby's relative health. The rating is based on five categories where the baby can score from 0 to 2 for each category, with the highest score being a cumulative score of ten. The categories and points include:

* Appearance (0 — The baby is blue, 1 — the baby has blue hands or feet, 2 — the baby is a normal color)

* Pulse (0 — Below 60 beats per minute, 1 — 60 to 100 beats per minute, 2 — greater than 100 beats per minute)

* Grimace (0 — No response to stimulation, 1 — slight reaction to stimulation 2 — a clear reaction to stimulation)

* Respiration (0 — Not breathing, 1 — weak cry, 2 — strong cry)

* Muscle tone (0 — Limp, 1 — reserved motion, 2 — active motion)

The most confusing of these categories is 'Grimace.' All it means is that the baby is showing a reaction to a reflexive stimulus like a gentle pinch or another discomfort. This is hardly high science and does not require medical tools.

Your doctor or nurse will likely offer a vitamin K shot for the baby, another thing you should decide long before it happens. Vitamin K is important for blood clotting and the baby's levels of this vitamin will typically be low, especially immediately after birth. The shot is known to decrease the possibility of haemorrhagic disease (a serious and potentially fatal bleeding condition). There are negligible risks associated with the shot and no known allergies. The worst thing that can happen is bruising at the injection site (usually the leg). Drops are available, but they have proven to be less effective than the shot and must be administered several times to be effective at all.

As things calm down, the reality of having created a new life will begin to sink in. You may want to make a few phone calls just to announce the newborn news to family or close friends. But it is probably more important for you to remain in the moment and share the experience with your partner and the child in your first moments as a family. This is not a performance that gets repeated and if you blink, you might miss it.

Not long after things become tranquil and the doctors and nurses file away, you will have the opportunity to witness the possibly awkward and beautiful first attempts at your partner breastfeeding your child. While it seems like it should be the most simple and natural thing on the planet because it has been going on since the beginning of the human race, breastfeeding may not be simple or automatic. The child's motor skills are brand new to them, and your partner has never had the opportunity to practice as a nursemaid. The harmony and comfort in the experience is as clumsy as a boy asking a girl to the dance floor for that first dance.

If all goes well, the bedlam of cries and complaining will turn to the practical silence of suckling. But if it does not — and don't expect it to — the frustrations of your partner and the hunger pangs of your baby will steadily mount with time. That time is measured in minutes rather than hours and days. It may not come easily, and there may need to be more than one attempt at the initial feeding, but with patience, it will come.

Depending on the time spent in delivery, you may be exhausted and irritable, but this is a moment where your strength and stoicism needs to shine. Your partner will be far more battered by the struggles of the episode than you and you need to be supportive of her efforts just as you have been supporting her during the pregnancy. You've only got to hold it together for a little while longer as your break is coming soon.

Many hospitals will have support services to coach your partner in the initial attempts at breastfeeding. If a lactation consultant is available, there is no reason to wait to engage their services. It can be a comfort to your partner and the baby to have a consultation — even if everything seems to be going well — just to be sure the nursing experience is optimal. Specific details in positioning can make the difference between functional feeding and being proficient.

As the baby feeds, a coach may promote more skin-to-skin contact. This has various advantages, including calming the child, elevating the chances of successful feeding and helping to regulate body temperature. As that first feeding progresses, you can watch the baby melt into a sense of calm. The wriggling, complaining and clenched fists come gradually to rest as the tight little fingers begin to open and relax. After this feeding, it is usually time for a nap.

You may have felt some distance from the immediacy and reality of your new situation throughout the experience of the pregnancy, but now it will begin to sink in and feel very real. Your baby may be more familiar with you and your partner than you know as they can hear your muffled voices in the womb. They probably won't see you very well at all as controlling any and all parts of themselves is a bit of an evolution. Continue to talk to them and get up close when you have the opportunity. The more you reinforce your presence, the quicker they will come to accept it. In that area, mom clearly has the upper hand.

You Might Go Home Alone

Your partner and the baby will stay at the hospital for at least a day or two following the birth. The inpatient care time will vary depending on the circumstances. For example, if the delivery was by c-section or episiotomy[1])or there were other complications, the stay may be longer. Some hospitals are set up so fathers can also stay for the duration, but that will vary from hospital to hospital and it should be something you have on your discovery list when you take a tour of the hospital.

Whether you have to leave or stay, it may be a good time to review any photos you took if you had the presence of mind to take any during the event. It may not only help you wind down, but you can make sure that you have them arranged in a way that is viewer friendly — especially if there are photos that other people really don't need to see. You want to do something pretty simple as you relax, and reliving the adventure may give you an idea of the photos you missed and may still have the chance to take, like with doctors and nurses or maybe some early family shots.

Whatever you choose to do, don't do it while driving home. Concentrate on the road. You should not be tempted to text people about the news while driving. You will probably feel a little exhausted if you don't already, and your family needs you to get home safely. Turn on some music or listen to anything that might keep you awake.

If you have some swing time to be alone between trips back to the hospital, it might be a good idea to continue the quest you started during the pregnancy as a super-partner. Assuming you have been good to your partner throughout the pregnancy, you have already

---

[1] an incision between the vagina and anus that expands the opening for the baby to pass through

15

created some habits you want to maintain. Being there for your partner — especially in the weeks after the birth — is something you will need to concentrate on, especially if it was a difficult birth. When you are with your partner and the child, hop in to change diapers. Beyond setting up some very practical things like getting necessities, you probably haven't thought much about dividing up the new responsibilities that come with a baby. Responsibility sharing will depend a lot on work commitments and how much you accomplished during the pregnancy to look ahead. In any case, this is definitely the time to start thinking about what matters now that you have successfully navigated the pregnancy.

If you left your house in a rush after the waters broke, look around to see what you can do so that your partner comes home to a clean house. Do routine chores like washing dishes, mowing the lawn, vacuuming, or sweeping. Start looking around the house for things that need childproofing and make a list. You will have a while before that needs to be completely taken care of, but taking it a little at a time will help you keep sane. You can also do it in stages to cover crawling or scooting, standing, and walking. My eldest walked early, at about six months. I'm pretty sure it was more dangerous than the youngest who scooted for almost two years. Looking back it was highly reflective of their personalities.

Baby-proofing Your Home

A lot of things that once seemed harmless to you are going to turn out not to be. The most obvious things you will want to invest in are baby-proof electrical outlet covers (make sure they are not a potential choking hazard) and cabinet and drawer locks. You might want to look at a few options because some are more convenient for you and safer for the baby. Designs may be dictated by the handles on the cabinets and drawers. Corner

---

guards for sharp furniture might save a whack on the head and inconsolable crying.

The other wise investments will be in baby gates for every room that will have to remain off-limits and any stairways — often top and bottom. This is another component of baby-proofing where the designs might make a lot of difference. For example, if either parent has mobility concerns, you may not want a gate you must step over. Gates you must remove often need to be put back quickly and firmly. Using the excuse, "it'll only be a second," is never reliable. Whatever you buy needs to be secure and safe for the whole family. Check with consumer reports and parenting sites.

Look around at your low shelves for any knickknacks, fancy plates, books, bottles, medicines, cleaners, chemicals and pet food that need to be moved to higher shelves. It may be silly, but crawling around your home might get you a few laughs, a little exercise, and a baby's-eye view of potential dangers. You'll spot electrical cords that dangle, waiting to be pulled. They all need to be shortened and tucked securely away. Watch out for where you charge portable devices.

Things you might not typically consider may also need to be dealt with. Unsecured furniture and shelving units might need a bracket to permanently secure them to the wall. Got a nice expensive large-screen TV? It needs to be braced if it isn't already.

Other than that, consider plants, your store of plastic shopping bags, any rocking or moving chairs, toy safety (e.g., materials used, potential choking hazards) and faucet covers (to prevent accidental baby burns). A must is investing in a baby monitor and keeping the crib clear of plush things (from pillows to stuffed animals and bumper pads). Many studies show they are not a good idea and could be a hazard.

Surviving the first 24 hours with your newborn will be filled with brand-new experiences. Drink them in and learn what you can about the person who has suddenly become a very real new member of your family. You and your partner will need to work together and be wholly responsible for many years. Right now, the child is the most vulnerable and least able to take care of themselves. The bigger problem is that you'll be responsible for providing the basic things your baby needs, and you may have absolutely no experience doing that. This is why the next chapter will dive deeper into that subject.

Dad Hacks From Chapter 1

Baby Prep Hack #1: Think Like a Baby. When it comes to baby proofing, you can't be too careful. While it may be a bit before your child can roam freely, you'll want to lock down every part of your home as soon as possible. Your bedroom, your bathroom, the kitchen, the living room; find every corner, chemical, and crevice that your baby could possibly get into.

Baby Prep Hack #2: Your Newborn May Look Odd; That's Okay! Babies can look very strange when they are first born, but there is no reason to worry. Your baby may have bent legs or feet, puffy/swollen eyes, and may even have a blue or purplish hue. Remember, your partner has just been through a very challenging event; freaking out about how the baby looks will not help. If you are concerned, talk to your doctor, but for the most part, your baby will look "normal" within 24 hours.

Baby Prep Hack #3: Skin-to-Skin Contact is Important. Skin-to-skin contact is essential between the mother and baby in the first hour after birth. If your partner is unable to facilitate this contact, you will have to do it yourself. Skin-to-skin contact after the birth is a huge boost to bonding. Hold your baby and make eye contact with them; this will help them feel safe and calm.

Baby Prep Hack #4: Make Sure Your Partner Gets Rest. Your partner will be physically and emotionally drained after birth, and they will need help getting proper rest in order to recover. Try to take the reins of baby care in the first 48 hours while your partner gets an opportunity to relax and get their strength back. Taking care of diapers, helping with feeding, and tending to your partners needs will go a long way to getting them back on their feet.

Baby Prep Hack #5: Discuss Breastfeeding. Breastfeeding can be difficult at first, and your partner will need reassurance if the baby is having trouble latching. You can consult specialists at the hospital, a lactation consultant, or your primary GP for advice on how to help your partner. They will be emotionally raw, so make sure to take responsibility for finding these specialists and fixing the problem A.S.A.P.

Chapter 2

Basic Care for Your Baby

"More often than not, the secret of success lies in the very basic, the very small wins. The small, consistent and disciplined steps lead to big successes."
— *Abhishek Ratna*

Now that you got your baby home, a bigger challenge begins. Learning to raise your baby will be a work in progress regardless of how much you have read and studied. There is no rush to become an expert at everything. There are some more significant mistakes you'll want to avoid, but you don't need to sweat the small stuff. Take small steps to learn a little at a time, and expect to goof some things up. Always keep in mind that you have a partner to lean on for help.

The first potential error you want to avoid is not treating the newborn gently enough. It is a little like a china doll. This is especially true for babies before they develop neck strength and other associated motor skills. You must support the head when holding the baby and in every position. If you don't, it can easily flop and cause injury. Be mindful that the head can flop in any direction, so you must protect it from all angles.

Cradling the baby in your arm is one good way to prevent any problems, but remain aware of head and neck at all times, including when feeding, burping, and changing. At times it may be more comfortable and practical to support with a firm hand on the back of the neck. That says 'firm' and not 'forceful.' Too much pressure might be as bad as too little. When putting the baby down to change its diaper, placing it into a carriage, car seat, or another carrier may be the least comfortable because you will be holding the baby away from you to place it down. This is where you will support it with your hand behind the neck just below the skull with your open palm. Squirming might make this a little tricky. Take your time. There is not a lot that is good about dropping the baby. There is absolutely no room for rough play.

Try not to forget about the importance of sanitation. The baby will have antibodies and an immune system, but it will not yet be well-developed. We are probably all more well-aware than we'd like to be of the importance of keeping your hands clean because of the experience with the pandemic. Maintaining a good regimen of washing your hands or using sanitizer before handling the baby makes a lot of sense. You may notice that doctors wash their hands a lot during your baby visits. That isn't just obsessive-compulsive disorder (OCD). It is good practice. You will also want to maintain a regimen for the baby when changing and after feeding.

Always make sure the baby is strapped into carriers and that you are using infant-appropriate devices. Anything that makes them sit up too straight in these early weeks will not be ideal. Read the instructions. There will be safety tips that are important to digest and best practices to follow. If you buy something used, request the user's manual or check to see if you can find one online. Carry out checks of the ground underfoot; for example, if you are holding a baby carrier seat and walk out on some black ice, that may be a disaster. You also want to be careful if you go out to the supermarket. Stacking a carrier on top of a shopping cart is not a good idea. On the other hand — and I am hoping it is unnecessary to say this — don't leave the baby in the car.

If you or your partner can't manage to go food shopping safely, make up a list with your partner and volunteer to get it done while she cares for the child. Don't forget to list brand names and sizes. If you have ever been sent out to buy feminine hygiene products, you may be familiar with the unfamiliar wall of choices. I had that experience and with no idea what to do. I just watched other shoppers for a few minutes picking things out, looked for places where the shelves were depleted and made the best guess. Of course, I came home with the wrong item and was sent back to the store. This can happen with anything. If you don't take notes and your list says 'cereal', coming home with Captain Crunch instead of Cheerios will find you slogging back to the market again.

Changing a Diaper

This is probably part of being a dad that it is difficult to look forward to. Once you get used to it and work out a regimen, it becomes second nature, and it really isn't as awful as you might think in concept.

Before bringing the baby home, you should have already decided whether to use cloth or disposables. Some people like the simplicity of disposables, but it may be interesting to look into diaper services which I found to be about the same price. It is far more environmentally friendly than plastic diapers that will last forever. My spouse and I used a combination of cloth for regular use and disposables in the diaper/travel bag. The reason is the cloth has to be emptied and sometimes rinsed before going into the wash hamper. Not very easy to do when you are out at a store.

Whatever your choice, you have to learn to work with it. Disposables were easy to put on and dispose of. The cloth frightened me initially because I feared jabbing the baby with the giant safety pins. Practice will get you everywhere.

Keep your supplies loaded wherever you plan to do most of your changing. It is not OK to leave the baby unattended on a changing table so you can hunt for supplies. You obviously need diapers and extra pins if you are using cloth. Keeping ointment and diaper wipes on hand is good because you will need both to wipe up. A towel or other cloth diaper should probably go under the baby to quickly work out 'accidents'. If you change a boy, you may be in for a fountain when you get the diaper off. It is wise to be ready in self-defense. A container to dispose of used diapers and wipes is also a good idea. Your diaper bag should be just as well-equipped.

To change the diaper — whether #1 or #2 — you want the baby on its back. As you peel off the diaper, don't be in a hurry, as you may not know precisely what you will uncover. You can use a washcloth or wipes to remove any residual mess. When changing a girl, wipe from front to back to avoid causing urinary tract infections (UTIs). Rashes can occur even if you are good at keeping up with diaper changes. I applied ointment every time to be proactive about rashes. That doesn't have to be a special product. For example, Vaseline works in a pinch. Diaper rash can become severe and get infected if left untreated. Wash your hands after changing, just like you would when visiting the bathroom.

If diaper rash happens, it may make the baby uncomfortable. It is just another reason for new opportunities to cry. Make an effort to be sure the child's little parts are clean after a change. Be gentle wiping the rash, be sure that ointment is applied and that you don't allow diaper changes to go over-long. You may change the baby about every hour of the day, including in the middle of the night. It may be good to check more frequently if a rash appears. A rash does not mean you've done anything wrong. The baby's skin is sensitive and some babies are more sensitive than others. If the rash does become infected (bleeding lesions), it is time for a trip to the doctor.

Bathing the Baby

Bathing your baby doesn't have to be more frequent than about twice a week unless there is a particularly explosive diaper. In the first few weeks, while you wait for circumcision to heal or the umbilical cord to fall off, it is best not to bathe the baby in a tub or sink. Doing so could interfere with the natural healing. Planning bath days can help reduce the risk of rashes. But bear in mind bathing is a double-edged sword. Too few baths and you risk a rash. Too many, and you risk drying out the baby's delicate skin.

Baths should be brief early on. There isn't a lot to wash anyway. This is probably best done with a washcloth and a very gentle soap — like those made for babies. Don't go hard on the soap and be sure the water temperature is lukewarm. Hot water can easily scald the baby so test it as you would with milk on your wrist or elbow. Having a plastic cup of some kind can help when rinsing the baby's hair and pouring water over the body, so the baby doesn't get cold. Go at everything gently, but wipe down all the little crevices behind the ears and the pudgy folds behind the legs. It is a good idea to clean the eyes, nose and ears, but don't use soap or anything 'clever' like Q-Tips.

If you use a baby tub, only fill it a few inches and be sure the water is off before placing the baby in the water. Leaving it running could alter the water temperature, or a distraction might find the water level too high.

When you are finished doing the simple wipe down, get the baby out of the water and into a towel to dry them off. The baby might tend to be slippery when wet — all the more reason to be extra careful. Be gentle rubbing the top of the head as the skull cap will not be fully formed and there is a soft spot. Don't press that, as the baby's delicate little brain is below. Dry the baby thoroughly. Then you might hit any areas that look red with a gentle ointment. Get that diaper on and swaddle to ensure the baby is not cold.

Dealing with Crying

One of the most challenging things about parenting a newborn is they can't tell you what they want. They sort of do, but not with words. Crying is a language, and you may get to understand how your baby is talking to you with a bit of time and patience. Babies will not all speak the same language, but you should begin to understand them after a while. A shrieking means something very different to a low-toned cry. In no particular order, crying can be due to various stressors:

- *Boredom.* Under-stimulation by being left too long alone without visual, sound or sensation of motion. The baby craves human contact and entertainment; without this, they may resort to whining as a way to self-soothe.
- *Pain.* Overfeeding can cause distension or excessive gas. It might be that the baby needs to be burped. Be sure to put on a shoulder rag if you go this route because whether the cause is too much milk or too much air, you can't predict which will come up. But there can be many sources of pain, some more or less obvious. An earache, mouth sores, urinary tract infection, constipation, or raw rash could make the baby cry out.
- *Hunger.* Probably the greatest cause of crying is hunger. In these early months the baby will need to eat often. While

similar to pain in that they feel discomfort, there is one relatively easy solution to hunger, whereas pain can be trickier to resolve.

- *Needing sleep.* When your baby can't get to sleep, you may need to work on your scheduling and not let waking periods go over time—having too many visitors who want to see the baby can unintentionally trigger that. But there are also methods to calm your baby and help them enter a restful sleep.
- *Sickness.* If your baby contracts an illness and gets a fever, like you, they might have a headache and sore throat. Watch out for signs of a high fever which is considered 100.4°F/38°C. You will want to take a trip to the doctor above that temperature to find out the cause.
- *Dirty diaper.* This is probably number two on the list of uncomfortable infants. Keeping excreted matter against the skin for extended periods will make the baby uncomfortable, whether the diaper is wet or otherwise. They will let you know that they are.
- *Mother's diet.* If the mother continues to breastfeed by whatever method (pump or breast to mouth), the mother's diet may affect the child. For example, if mom consumes caffeine regularly, the child may have difficulty sleeping. Even if her diet is mostly healthy and one or two habits don't agree with the child, there may be adverse reactions.

Other stressors may contribute to crying, but these are some of the most common causes. The list does not end there. If you really pay attention, you might learn by listening to the baby monitor what solution your baby needs. Start your diagnosis with this list.

When your baby starts crying — and it is when not if — stay calm. It is probably nothing that you are doing wrong. It will probably be frustrating, especially if it goes on for an extended period of time.

You may need to put the baby down and let them cry while you go into another room and breathe. But there are methods you can find that work.

It is always good to check the simple things first, like hunger and their diaper. These are the easiest to fix. But think before jumping to any conclusions. For example, the problem is probably not hunger if the baby was just fed. After checking the diaper, it is perhaps best to consider burping even if you already did it. This does more than one thing as it comforts the baby in the stomach to chest body contact. If the baby is already with you, it is probably not boredom. They probably need to sleep if they have been up for an unusually long time.

What I am saying is keep a list (even if it is in your head) and start by eliminating what the problem shouldn't be. Take note of the things that work in solving the issue when you get the baby to stop crying and be ready to use them again. One method will probably not work the same way every time, but there are a lot of potential solutions to consider. Two of the best are motion and sound or even a combination.

Motion

Motion can successfully calm a baby — especially if you don't know the source of the issue —. Taking the baby out for a walk in the stroller can often soothe savage tantrums. I discovered by accident that walking in a gravel parking lot calmed my eldest when I tried to take a shortcut. The ride was a little bumpy, but I am betting the white noise of the stones grinding under the tires also helped get her to sleep. I put that solution in my pocket and used it often. Hopefully, the neighbors don't complain.

Strapping baby in a car seat and going on a drive is a suggestion that a lot of experts mention. The theory is that the low-frequency vibrations from the sound of the motor and wheels on the road can be soothing. Also, the baby gets moved to a different environment, there isn't a ton of stimulation in the back seat of a car, and there is a change of scenery. Even adults sometimes fall asleep from the motion of a vehicle. Just be sensible and don't go out driving when you are over-tired. In that case, it may be best to sit with the baby in a rocking chair or put it in a baby swing. The simple motion might be just the remedy to put the baby to sleep.

Noise

A popular phrase used in some households was: "Be quiet. The baby's sleeping." Mothers or fathers exhausted from getting their baby to sleep just weren't ready to have the baby wake up again. But noise can work in several different ways. Some can help you get your baby to sleep; others may cover background noise so life can go on in the household without tiptoeing around.

Music just may become your best friend—some kids like classical music and some like metal. Of course, there are lullabies and music considered to be for children. It is a bit of a trial-and-error process. Some children fall asleep or at least calm down to the sound of white noise. It sounds like turning on the shower or setting a radio to a channel that doesn't exist. Brown noise may be a better option as it is a lower frequency. Both can be useful in drowning out background noise in the house. More unusual options for sleep induction have to do with binaural beats (tone and frequency recordings). The internet offers many options for more natural noise, like rain storms. Similar to white and brown noise, the sounds of nature can be soothing for some babies.

The key to using sound or motion — or both simultaneously — is distracting the baby from the issue that is bothering them. Doing your best to diagnose the reason for crying will ultimately be the most effective way to resolve things. If the baby is already over-stimulated, it does not make sense to use a solution that will stimulate them more. If they are bored and overtired, a change in scenery might be all they need to change their mood.

Another Option for Sleep

Techniques for hypnosis can also be effective in getting babies to relax into a deep sleep. It seems they only work on babies ready to fall asleep, not those crying. Something that may be worth looking into are techniques based on Franz Mesmer's practices, developed 200 years ago. They are straightforward methods for helping your baby relax. The following is a good resource produced by an award-winning hypnotherapist. https://youtu.be/qZn6Nd0bG5k

---

Bonding with Your Baby

Making an effort to bond with your baby has a lot of benefits. First, it is necessary to begin forming your personal relationship with your new baby. Second, it can be comforting and soothing for the baby, which will help reduce crying episodes. Third, your partner will notice your effort, and that can very well enhance your relationship.

Bonding with your child begins almost immediately after birth. As it is a non-verbal process, you will not be communicating with words. You start creating your connection with touch, gesture and other physical actions. Voice does play a role, but it isn't exactly the one you may think.

The physical aspect starts with just holding your child, which is why it is essential to get comfortable. When you are uncomfortable, you subconsciously communicate with a vibe that says you are uncertain and perhaps even "I don't like this." Not the kind of message you want to begin communicating.

Your partner will have a huge advantage in her opportunities to connect with the child. She already has. Before the baby is even born, there is a connection formed through carrying the baby for nine months. But even immediately after birth, she has the chance to breastfeed, and that type of contact is something the dad will not have the opportunity to do. Well, at least not exactly.

An alternative to breastfeeding is taking the opportunity to bottle feed when that is an option. It is possible, for example, to pump breast milk and use it in bottles allowing you intermittent opportunities to feed the baby. Like your partner's first attempts at breastfeeding, bottle feeding might not go particularly well, especially if your partner is exclusively breastfeeding without a bottle. If it doesn't go well, it may work for the mom to introduce occasionally feeding with a bottle just to make the child feel comfortable with the new format. When it goes well with her, chances are that the dad has a greater probability of being able to pull it off.

Feeding is just one example of making the child accept and bond with you. It is not the be-all-and-end-all.[2] Even if the bottle feeding does not go well right away, you can take the time to practice holding the child in comforting ways. The better you get at assuming a position of nursing (cradling for bottle feeding), the more likely you will succeed with the bottle. But you will want to practice other positions, like chest-to-chest contact. You can practice making the

---

[2] An interesting study on the subject of bonding was a series of experiments conducted by psychologist Harry Harlow in 1958 on rhesus monkeys. In part of the series of experiments, Harlow separated newborns from their mothers and placed them with two surrogate mothers. One of the mothers was made of wire and provided only food. The other was wrapped in something like fur, which the monkeys could 'cuddle'. The infant monkeys spent more time with the cuddly mom than the one that fed them. It is worth looking at the study. https://www.simplypsychology.org/harlow-monkey.html

baby feel safe in your arms during these sessions. You might even try some gentle massaging and stroking.

Another way to enhance the connection with your newborn is to talk. You don't have to use words, light singing, cooing or even humming will serve the purpose. Any vocal sounds that will help get the baby used to hearing your voice can help you make this type of connection. But there is also no reason you can't tell the child stories, read books with them, or tell them about the world around them as you take them on a stroll. You will just want to be mindful of not startling the baby with a booming voice, or you may set off a crying session. But the point here is that familiarity brings comfort, trust, and bonding.

Basic care of your baby has to do as much with paying attention to your needs as well as the child's. Stepping up to go the extra mile and evolving your efforts with time makes you more inclusive in the family. The whole experience may be new to you, but this chapter should have provided some perspective on the very basics of caring for the child and making yourself welcome in their lives. You should know how to avoid grave errors, change a diaper, bathe the baby, deal with crying, and make attempts to start bonding. Of course, this is just a starting place, as your experience has to be felt out with some trial and error.

We touched on feeding here, and there is a bit more to it. That is why we look at feeding in more depth in Chapter 3.

Dad Hacks From Chapter 2

Basic Care Hack #1: Handle With Care. Just like shipping a rare vase, handling your baby should be done with the utmost care. Make sure to support your baby's head and neck every time you pick them up. If you have to bend down, make sure to bend your knees and pull the baby close to your chest.

Basic Care Hack #2: Soothing and Bonding Go Hand-in-Hand. Bonding with your baby helps them feel safe around you, and will teach them to seek you out when they feel in danger. Try different methods of soothing your baby while holding them close; all babies are unique, and your child may need to be calmed down with a variety of methods.

Basic Care Hack #3: Practice Your Diaper Change to Save Time. Like a one-man formula one pit crew, you'll want to get your diaper changing down to a science. Practice your technique, and take every opportunity to give your partner a break by changing diapers yourself. Not only will they appreciate it, but you'll be able to get faster at the change and save yourself time.

Basic Care Hack #4: Don't Let Crying Get to You. It's okay to get frustrated when your baby won't stop crying. Take a second, give yourself a moment outside with some silence (provided your partner can watch the baby), then go back in and find out the reason for their crying. Babies can cry because they are hungry, tired, have a dirty diaper, are adjusting to temperature, need to burp, and a million other reasons. Try to find your baby's frequent cry triggers and act accordingly to fix the problem.

Basic Care Hack #5: It's Okay To Call the Doctor. Some people worry they will be bothering their doctor, but anxiety in the first few months can be overwhelming. Don't hesitate to contact your doctor if you believe there are any problems at all with your baby. Yes, that means on occasion you will go in and they will say "they just have gas" or "they have a very slight fever." But it's better to be safe than sorry, and checking will help you sleep easier at night!

Chapter 3

How to Feed Your Baby the Right Way

"Nourishment comes in many forms. So does happiness." — *Ranjani Rao*

Nutrition is not something that simply satiates hunger. For your baby to grow in mind and body, develop properly, and set the stage for a healthy life, you need to feed your baby correctly. They obviously will not make any choices for themselves, so this is your responsibility. They may be able to turn on the alarm and cry when hungry, but they won't even know what they want, let alone understand what the practical options are. Baby is not going to be in the highchair throne chomping steak or wielding the handle of a turkey leg like Henry VIII anytime soon (although they will command the attention of the room like they are holding court before long).

In this chapter, we look at the idea of schedules for eating during the baby's first year and the dos and don'ts as far as what you should allow to pass their lips during their stages of development. It is good enough to tackle the basics in the beginning, to get by as you settle into a routine. You will have certain rules to follow for health and safety. But as your parenting skills increase, so should your approach to nutrition.

What's on the Menu

It probably seems impossible to an adult how little sustenance your baby actually needs in the first weeks of life. It is not more by volume than you can fit into one mouthful of your chosen drink. That volume is per feeding. This may make you wonder about the initial fuss over getting breastfeeding right because nothing much is being consumed anyway. The small initial volume is part of the reason why it isn't urgent to get it right the first time. But the need for frequency (about ten times a day) is why it is essential to work at solving any problems right away.

When the baby was in utero, they were getting nurtured constantly. Now, with a stomach about the size of a marble, they have to start to be at least partly responsible for their own subsistence (they must at least swallow). They really should not go more than four hours without feeding. While their stomach will increase in size fairly rapidly — probably quadrupling in capacity in the first two weeks — that is still just about two fluid ounces per feeding.

Expected Milk Intake by Average (Feeding and Frequency)
   Newborn to 2 weeks: .5 to 2 oz. (on demand)
   2 weeks to 2 months: 3 oz. (8X per day)
   2 to 4 months: 5 oz. (7X per day)
   4 to 6 months: 6 oz. (7X per day)
   6 to 12 months: 8 oz. (6X per day)
   12+ months: 8+ oz. (4X per day)
Keep in mind that these are ballpark numbers. You will have to adjust to your baby (e.g. If your baby is very small, the intake will be less). The whole schedule and list of expectations may be tossed on its head should your baby be born prematurely.

Choices about breastfeeding, using breast milk, or bottle-feeding with formula are personal. However, the choice to do one or the other is not always driven by a simple selection. Some factors can filter into the equation that may be beyond your control. Either way, making an informed choice means knowing why you'd select one over the other in the first place.

One curious fact about your baby and liquids is that baby should only be consuming breast milk or formula for the first year. Juice, cow's milk and even water are not recommended as they do not provide the right nutrients and won't be helpful to the baby's health and development, which are critical concerns — especially in the first year. You will be introducing solids sometime around the sixth month. There is no need to rush to that, and you will continue feeding milk/formula when the solids are introduced.

Whatever you do, pay attention to the recommendations of your pediatrician. The information here is a rough guide and not the ultimate one.

Breastfeeding

One of the tricky things about breastfeeding is you have no idea how much the baby is supping per feeding. You can be assured it isn't much in those first two weeks, and most people will find early bottle feeding not worth the effort. However, not everyone has the same interest in continuing to breastfeed or in choosing breastfeeding at all.

Before talking about bottle feeding, there are some benefits of breastfeeding over the long term to mention. Breast milk is nature's natural nectar. Evolution provides mom with the best factory for providing nutrition to her baby. Mom's milk churns out with the perfect balance of nutrients from fats and protein, plus the fluid is packed with easily digestible vitamins, trace elements and antibodies. The only caveat here is that the quality of the milk depends on the mother's diet. A well-balanced diet that limits junk food and promotes good nutrition delivers the fuel the body needs to manufacture infant-nourishing milk.

Breast milk will be easier for the baby to digest than formula. It will be supportive of all systems and functions, supportive of healthy development, and the baby will get a steady stream of beneficial bacteria to develop their intestinal flora. The nutritional benefits help boost a baby's immune system and lower the likelihood of developing allergies, ear infections and gastrointestinal issues. No matter how well 'formulated', formula doesn't do all these things. Starting your child with the ultimate food source can prepare your child for a long, healthy life. As long as mom takes a little care with what she is ingesting, there are clear nutritional benefits. Don't smoke, drink, or overdo things (e.g., caffeine, herbal supplements, fish with high mercury content, or highly processed foods).

Breast milk is always ready at the perfect temperature and in the ideal volume in the ultimate juice box. There is no need to head off to the kitchen, worry about cleaning bottles, and potential problems with 'food management' (things don't keep in the fridge forever) or sterilization. Baby takes what baby wants, and there is virtually zero waste. It is free.

One more little consideration is the benefit for mom. Milk production burns calories. The weight gained during pregnancy (all women gain during pregnancy) will be lost much faster. There are also other health benefits that may be worth researching, such as a lowered chance of developing diabetes and breast or cervical cancer.

Bottle Feeding

While the benefits of breastfeeding seem evident, there are some valid reasons why a new mom might choose to go to formula quickly

— or even immediately. Bottle feeding is not necessarily independent of breastfeeding as some women may choose to pump and store their milk for bottle feeding just for the convenience of not having to always be the one responsible for the feeding. But for the sake of simplicity, 'bottle feeding' in this section refers to formula.

Some matters of convenience or practicality have people choose to go directly to bottle feeding. Not all of them are selfish or ill-advised, and they may not be steering away from what is best for the baby despite the numerous advantages of breast milk.

In rare cases, children are born lactose intolerant, which would have essentially been fatal before the availability of formula. Parents can consider substitutes, like soy milk, to bottle-feed the baby. Whether the choice to bottle-feed has a medical basis or not, bottle-feeding allows the responsibility of feeding to be shared between parents far more easily. This can help the dad bond with the child during feedings from a very early stage in a way that isn't otherwise possible. The responsibility is also not limited to the parents so that a village can help raise the child if needed.

Feeding with formula will tend to leave your baby full longer. This is partly because formula will be more difficult to digest, so it stays in the stomach longer. This comes along with the benefit of less frequent feedings. It could lead to increasing the baby's stomach capacity at a faster rate which in turn leads to needing to feed more per feeding and possibly enhanced weight gain.

Bottle feeding can be done anywhere, whereas breastfeeding can sometimes be a little awkward — no matter how normal it should otherwise be. Some cultures (e.g., the USA) will have more issues with open breastfeeding. Bottles also make it easier to measure how much your baby consumes. This also separates any concern about what mom is ingesting. Sometimes mom's personal situation can mean choosing a bottle. For example, if the mother needs treatment for a condition with medications. Medications will leech into the milk production and dose the infant as well.

Sanitation of baby bottles is critical. You want to make an effort to keep to hospital standards without dousing everything in chemicals, as chemicals do more harm than good. Optimally, you want to clean bottles immediately after you have finished using them so nothing has the opportunity to crust inside. Avoid making silly mistakes like using an old smelly sponge to do the 'cleaning.' Use a bottle brush and wash the bottles thoroughly with hot water (boiling all the bottles for regular sterilization is a good idea). Clean your bottle brush after each use as well. Read the manufacturer's instructions for proper care of your specific product.

The bottles are not the only place you need to sanitize. Regardless of what you think of your water source, you need to boil the water before mixing formula. Boil it and let it cool. While it isn't an issue if you mix bottle-by-bottle by shaking in the bottle itself, pay attention to the utensils you use to make the formula. For example, if you use a kitchen utensil to mix formula for the day (perhaps a whisk or a spoon), sterilize it beforehand by making sure it is clean and then boil the end in water for 2 minutes. Things can look clean, but it is not the things you can see that you are necessarily worried about. Err on the side of safety. Boiling water takes care of a lot of concerns. Be careful around boiling water, and don't bring the baby anywhere near it.

Introducing Solids

A few things are rough markers for when your baby is ready to start with solid foods. It could be as early as four months, but it will depend on various factors. At the very least, the baby must have good motor control of their head. They should have had good weight gain on their fluid diet (e.g., 50% weight gain from birthweight or more), and they might be showing an interest in food (reaching for solid food sources or watching intently as you eat). Other signs might include fist chewing and an increase in milk requests.

Once you decide to introduce solids, or when the doctor recommends it, plan to go slowly. Some basic warnings will help keep you out of trouble and your baby out of harm's way. Things that seem harmless additions to the baby's diet might be more like feeding chocolate to your dog. A dog will gladly take chocolate, just like your baby will start putting nearly anything in their mouth. It will not end well for the dog and could potentially kill them. You can figure out what I am inferring about the baby.

Few foods are banned from the infant's menu except for honey. Even dipping a finger in some honey to give your baby a taste of the yummy magic you may be using for its health benefits can wind up giving your child a case of infant botulism. If that sounds frightening, it should because complications can be life-threatening. The other potential source of this deadly toxin (botulinum is produced by clostridium botulinum) may include home-canned foods. It is a good reason not to feed your baby any well-meaning gifts of homemade baby foods, no matter how much you respect the person giving you the gift. While it may be impolite to refuse the gesture, utilizing them will probably be unwise and possibly life-threatening.

Along this line of thinking about foods with potentially harmful bacteria would fall any number of unpasteurized foods. These can contain even low levels of bacteria that an older child will just shrug off but still enough to infiltrate your baby's delicate immune system and create a bad situation. These same foods will be fine when that immune system is better established, but let it get established and until then, exercise caution. A good example of foods that seem harmless is cheese made with unpasteurized milk. This can easily sneak by you because most people think cheese is cheese. While most of these unpasteurized foods may be ultimately harmless, there is no reason in the world to take that risk when there are other safe choices. And, yes, this ultimately means you are going against the mantra of avoiding processed foods because pasteurizing is processing. However, you are generally turning toward foods processed specifically for infants' consumption, not the type of processed foods that get slammed by the media.

Foods with sugar and salt: both get a no. You may feel like you want the baby to experience culinary delights, but there is plenty of time for that. Salt can work against a baby's delicate metabolism and cause kidney damage. That is indeed frightening, especially when it is totally unnecessary to flavor their food. Avoiding sugar and any type of sweets for at least the first two years of development can save your baby from future health problems (there is a long list, including obesity, heart disease, high blood pressure, etc.). There is absolutely no reason the baby needs sugar in its diet. You might feel you want to give them a treat, and chances are they probably won't even like it because it may be overpowering. If they do, you may create a monster. It will be enough for them to get used to the sensation of having something other than fluid in their mouth.

One keyword to think about when it comes to your baby's diet: is bland. Imagine the scenario you are dealing with. Your baby has had nothing but air and milk until you go to introduce solid food. Getting used to swallowing solid food will be hard enough. Experiencing the invasion of a foreign substance into their oral cavity for the first time will be enough of a surprise. The reaction will probably be along the lines of electrifying their tongue and taste buds as they've been sleeping along on the same menu and flavors for six months or so. Taste buds are going to get their first test drive, and it won't take much to over-excite them. Go ahead and taste whatever it is you choose to give your baby first. It will be mushy and bland, and you probably won't like it. That's perfect.

Choking hazards are something to keep in mind. Anything that would typically require chewing is not a good idea to feed the baby. A key clue you should note is the baby's distinct lack of teeth. No teeth, no chewing. No chewing raises the choking hazard. People insist on making bad choices when it comes to this, like giving a baby a peanut. The baby is not an elephant, and your house is not a zoo. Don't do that. There are even soft foods that are not a particularly good idea. For example, jello, often considered a kid's favorite, is not for babies. They don't have to chew it as it will eventually melt in their mouth, but that's not the problem. The problem is that while it is in solid form, it can easily slide into their throat and stop the baby from breathing. That's a pretty serious consequence. It also puts aside the fact that jello is loaded with sugar, which you were already supposed to be avoiding. Donuts, no. Cakes, no. Everything needs to be mashed and sloppy — sometimes even what may seem like unpleasant slurry.

What you choose as a first food is less important than that it is simple, and the baby gets the idea of how the mechanism works. Try feeding solids for the first time before giving them a bottle. They will be more hungry at this time and willing to do more to quell that hunger. You should not force the baby's mouth open. If you take the usual path and get some kind of branded puree bland vegetable mush, get it on the spoon and let the baby offer by opening their mouth. Some pretty hysterical things can happen here, depending on the level of interest the baby has shown up to this point. They have likely been watching you eat, and mimicking is one of their preferred behaviors. If the baby isn't showing an interest as you proffer the mush on a spoon, show them how it is supposed to work. If they go to grab the spoon, let them guide it but don't let go. They might just grab what's in the spoon. Oh, well. You can't expect early attempts to go well or the mess to be contained. You can't guarantee that any will go in their mouths, either.

In the initial attempts, how much the baby eats is unimportant. They will still primarily get all their nutrition from formula/milk. You are working on creating a gateway to weaning. It does not happen all at once by any means. And really, you should only try once a day until there is progress. You may have to try this many times before it seems genuinely successful. You can meter success by the fact that something goes in and it doesn't come back out. Once the swallowing mechanism is mastered, you can start to vary the menu. There is no reason to rush and go too fast to a broad menu as there is no culinary demand from the baby. Every new food is an adventure.

Stay with mushy things. You might even let baby join in with a family meal by giving them mushy something. For example, if you are serving potatoes, let the baby have a little of it mashed. As the baby progresses, try giving them soft foods cut into small pieces. Once they handle that, give them things that are slightly more challenging. Plain Cheerios are a popular motor-skill builder. It is as simple as setting your baby up in a high chair and scattering a few Cheerios on the baby's tray. Letting them fuss and strain isn't cruel entertainment; it is helping them develop motor skills and hand-eye coordination.

Your confidence is as important as the baby's in handling what you give them. There is no real reason to hold them back from exploration as long as you are smart about the dietary choices. Keep things simple, flavor nothing, and bite sizes appropriate to their skills. Do experiment with soft foods like fresh fruits (e.g., banana, avocado), and roll out challenges a little at a time. Gradually move up to sizes baby can hold in their fist and bite off as they please.

Food Safety and Storage

To be sure that you do not create food hazards, be cautious about how you store food that your baby will be eating. If you buy baby food, check the cap on the jars before opening it by pressing the button on the lid down to check the seal. This helps you be sure that the jar didn't get opened previously in the store and that the content is not going bad (harmful bacteria can create gas, and the seal will become unstable). Once you open the jar, make sure it gets back in the fridge as soon as possible and plan to keep it for two days maximum.

There is no reason why you can't cook for a baby, but you need to be absolutely sure of your food safety practices. Anything you are cooking should be thoroughly cooked and well-cooled; when it comes to baby, think of pizza burning the roof of your mouth for everything more than slightly warm to the touch. Refrigeration is important, but you can make things worse by not doing it correctly. If you store food covered with plastic wrap or covered Tupperware, it should be cooled to 70° F/21° C before covering, or you create an environment for bacteria to thrive. Do not be casual with food safety practices, especially in the early going.

Much Ado About Water

You will not give your baby plain water in the first six months. They get all the hydration they need from their staple liquid diet. The other side is that giving them water early will deprive them of essential nutrition. Water will take up space they need for optimal nutrition.

At about six months, giving your baby small amounts of water as a stop-gap, a curiosity, and a learning tool is ok. This should always be cooled boiled water to ensure no chance of doing more harm than good, at least until the baby turns the corner at 12 months and the serious safety precautions can come off the table. Note that it says 'cooled'. Even if you boil it before refrigeration, ice water may be a bit of a shock. Your baby will not be able to describe 'brain freeze' to you, but their delicate system will be susceptible.

If you are concerned about hydration, a great barometer that will chase you throughout infancy is the number of wet diapers the baby has per day. If there are at least six reasonably wet diapers per day, your child is getting enough fluid. If it dips below there and your baby is maintaining its regular intake of milk/formula, you can consider offering water as a secondary source of hydration.

Juice becomes possible after 12 months, but the selection should be made with care. Most consumer juice products have a ton of sugar — which you want to avoid. Those that don't have chemical sweeteners (e.g., saccharine, high fructose corn syrup, sorbitol). Just because it doesn't say 'sugar' on the label — and it might even claim to be sugar-free — doesn't mean there aren't other harmful things mixed in to please the taste buds of average consumers. If you go the route of juice, stick with fresh orange juice or vegetable juices you make yourself by cooking fresh vegetables and pureeing them. Dilute any new introduction at first. If you do something silly like giving baby cabbage juice, the gastric distress may lead to hours of screaming and crying.

If your baby gets a fever, it is best to return to a strict and rather boring regimen of breast milk or formula. You may need to make feeding more frequent and expect the baby to take less volume each time. When sick, the baby will do far better on proven nutrition than with what will end up being less sustaining liquids.

***

Food is one of the basic necessities that deserves a deeper treatment. Sticking to advice that helps you keep things simple, sterile and progressive is definitely the best for the baby and probably you as well. The need for variety is not over-rated as it will teach your baby not to be too fussy about what gets put on their plate.

With nutrition under baby's belt, sleep is another big topic you must be concerned with for the baby's health and your own. Although we have covered some of the significant parts of the topic already, the next chapter rounds out the finer points of your baby's sleep regimen, so that night times go more smoothly.

Dad Hacks From Chapter 3

Feed Hack #1: Following a Schedule Can Reduce Stress. Setting up a schedule and adhering to it can take a lot of the guesswork out of feeding, helping alleviate stress that may be hindering both you and your partner. Set a timer between feedings to help you remember, though make sure the chime isn't too abrasive. No one wants to hear a blaring siren every 2 to 3 hours.

Feed Hack #2: It's Okay to Bottle Feed Occasionally. While there are some risks to bottle feeding, including the possibility of choking, ear infections, and tooth decay, it's okay to bottle feed from time to time. Bottle Feeding can give your partner's nipples a break and still give your baby the nutrients they need. Just make sure that the bottle is clean, and the baby never has it in their bed!

Feed Hack #3: No Water for the First 6 Months. It seems counterintuitive, but your baby should not have water during the first six months of their life. Baby's get all the nutrients and hydration they need from breastmilk and formula; giving them water can make them less thirsty for milk, which can stunt their

---

growth. Even on hot days (where you should be keeping your baby inside anyway) milk is all they need.

Feed Hack #4: There Will Be Foods Your Baby Hates. Once your baby switches to solids, there is one unfortunate fact to face: they will simply despite certain types of food. Try a variety of baby foods, and see if you can get a couple in rotation they enjoy. While you'll want to teach them later about the importance of trying new foods, the most essential thing in the first year is getting them the nutrients they need.

Feed Hack #5: Watch for Choking Hazards. You would be surprised at what qualifies as a choking hazard for your baby, and you'll want to keep your eyes (and carrots) peeled when watching out for potential choking danger. Even things like corn kernals, cherry tomatoes, and pieces of vegetables can choke your baby. Remember: food pieces larger than one half an inch (width or length) can cause your baby to choke.

Chapter 4

How to Help Your Baby Sleep

Sleep; babies need it, and parents wish they could have it. Unfortunately, only one of you will likely be getting proper rest, as studies have shown that new parents only get between 5 and 6 hours of sleep a night. But for your baby, losing sleep doesn't just mean being a bit irritable and needing an extra cup of tiny coffee. Sleep is the foundation of a baby's health; without proper rest, infants can suffer from problems later in life like:

- Decreased Brain Development
- Learning and Cognition Issues
- Frequent Negative Emotions
- Problems with Growth
- More Frequent Illness

It's estimated that a baby will wake up every two to three hours to feed, meaning that your sleep schedule will be somewhat erratic in the first few months of parenthood. Understanding the exact nature of these sleep patterns and how they change as the baby grows can help you overcome these nocturnal challenges (not to mention help you hold on to your sanity during the stress that sleeplessness can bring including not being able to binge watch Netflix! Or watch my favourite cat and dog videos on social media) I certainly struggled with this during those initial months with our first child, but over time, I learned effective ways to help our baby get the essential rest it needed. It may seem like an insurmountable challenge at first, but fortunately, there are a number of techniques you can use to make this process easier. We'll start by looking at the type of sleep patterns your baby will have during those first twelve months.

Understanding Infant Sleep Patterns

How your baby sleeps will change dramatically over the first twelve months of its life; we can separate this time into three distinct stages.

Stage 1: 0-3 Months

From that first night in the hospital to the first few months at home, a baby in its first three months of life will sleep for the majority of the day. Unfortunately, this sleep is rife with irregular patterns, and as much as parents would love to get some shut-eye themselves, babies won't always be tired at night. In any given 24-hour period, a baby less than three months old will sleep between 14 and 17 hours. Waking up every two to three hours to feed, it's not uncommon for a baby to wake up shortly after getting to sleep. Babies will nap frequently throughout the day, followed by a longer night-time sleep (if you are lucky!) The baby will also move around in their sleep, making small noises and even twitching. Their breathing can become irregular; fortunately, this is entirely normal, and there is no reason to respond unless the baby wakes up.

To sum up sleep patterns in the first three months:

- Your baby will sleep between 14 to 17 hours within a 24-hour period.
- The baby will wake up every two to three hours to feed.

- Babies at this stage do not have regular sleep patterns, so prepare for them to take several naps throughout the day.
- Babies are often in a stage of rest called "active sleep." They will move, twitch, make small noises like grunts, and even wake up briefly before returning to a quieter sleep stage.

Stage 2: 3-6 Months

After the first three months, the amount of sleep a baby needs will reduce slightly. In a 24-hour period, your average infant will rest between 12 to 16 hours, which includes periodic naps throughout the day. They will still need to be fed often and will wake up every few hours to satisfy their hunger. Luckily, their sleep cycle will start to become a bit more regular. They'll spend less time in active sleep (where they are twitching, moving, or grunting) and more time in the quiet rest we associate with deep sleep. They will also (thankfully) sleep for longer at night, staying awake longer during the day.

To sum up sleep patterns between months three and six:

- Your baby will sleep between 12 and 16 hours within a 24-hour period.
- The baby will still wake up every few hours to feed.
- Babies do have a more regulated sleep pattern during these months, staying awake during the day and sleeping longer at night.
- More time will be spent in quiet sleep rather than active, so your baby will move around and twitch far less than it did during the first three months.

Stage 3: 6 to 12 Months

During months six to twelve, your baby will maintain that 12 to 16-hour-a-day sleep pattern. They'll continue to take naps during the day, though these will decrease in frequency. Instead, your baby will nap for longer stretches, marked by less activity and more quiet sleep. A baby's sleep schedule becomes far more normalized during this time, and while they will still wake up at night to feed, they will do so more often during the day. Overall, you'll deal with far less sleep disturbance on your end, and more consistent, dependable sleep will occur.

To sum up sleep patterns between months six and twelve:

- Your baby will continue to sleep between 12 and 16 hours within a 24- hour period.
- The baby will still nap during the day, though far less frequently.
- Your baby will have much quieter sleep than the active sleep that causes them to twitch and move.
- Your baby will sleep more consistently at night, though they will still need to wake up occasionally to feed.

How Can I Be Sure My Baby Has Healthy Sleep?

Much like it is to adults, sleep is essential to maintaining your baby's good health. Understanding what constitutes healthy sleep patterns and identifying the signs of poor rest can help ensure your baby's development is not harmed during these crucial first months. First, you'll want to understand what it looks like when your baby needs more rest.

Signs That Your Baby Is Tired:

• Having trouble getting settled	• Tightening its fists
• Frequently yawning	• Jerking or moving around uneasily
• Rubbing their eyes	• Quiet while awake for long periods of time
• Crying, fussing, or visibly grimacing	• Not interested in playing

If you see one or more of these signs, it may be time to deploy a couple of sleep-improvement strategies. Babies need time to develop a healthy circadian rhythm, where they are mostly awake during the day and mostly asleep during the night. Even though this rhythm will take a bit to establish itself, there are a couple of ways you can accelerate the process.

Healthy Sleep Tips:

- *Natural Sunlight:* Humans are naturally attuned to sunlight, and studies have shown that our circadian clocks respond primarily to the presence of light and dark. When your baby wakes up in the morning, make sure to open up the blinds and expose them to as much natural sunlight as possible. Similarly, ensure that the room they sleep in is as dark as possible. These two light settings can help your baby develop their rhythm as early as possible when used in tandem.
- *Rock-a-Bye Baby:* It can be difficult for a fussy baby to drift off to sleep, especially if they had a particularly stimulating day. You can help ease your baby into their sleep schedule by soothing them with gentle rocking. Other techniques that

can make your baby a bit more sleepy include night-time feeding, singing to them softly, quietly shushing them as they fuss, or patting them as they begin to drift off.

- *Establish a Calming Routine:* Because we are trying to establish a rhythm, structuring bedtime around a routine can help your baby subconsciously know when it's time to go to sleep. Create a calming nightly ritual with activities like bath time, reading them a story, gentle massage, or the rocking/sleeping mentioned above. Keep this routine consistent, and before long, your baby will start to get tired before the routine has even finished.

Helping your baby nap can be accomplished with similar techniques, though the routines should be much shorter. For example, a short story or small snack before a nap can help your baby sleep more quietly, as well as putting them in the same spot (i.e. their crib) when it's time for them to rest.

Common Sleep Problems and How to Solve Them

Much like people of any other age, it's common for babies to have issues with sleeping from time to time. Different problems will occur at various times during infancy, and it can be frustrating when you aren't sure how to identify or deal with a specific issue. To figure this out, let's bring those stages from the earlier part of this chapter back and talk about a few of the sleep issues you'll face. Then, I'll show you the best way to deal with them so your baby (and you) can get some much needed shut-eye.

Sleep Problems in Stage 1: 0-3 Months

Issue: Back-Sleep Resistance

The safest way for a baby to sleep is on its back, but many infants will resist this positioning in an effort to get comfortable. Your baby will most likely prefer to sleep on his or her stomach, but studies have linked this sleeping position to higher instances of sudden infant death syndrome or SIDS.

How to Solve This Issue: To be as cautious as possible, the first step you should take is to talk to your paediatrician. It's possible that your baby may have some physical issue that is preventing it from back-sleeping comfortably; if that's the case, it should be addressed as quickly as possible. This may sound worrying, but it's just a precaution. More likely than not, your baby just doesn't feel secure sleeping on its back. If the doctor gives you the all-clear, you can encourage back sleeping by swaddling your baby and giving them a pacifier. These, and other comforting elements like reading to them at bedtime or feeding them before sleep, can make your baby feel secure in a back-sleeping position.

Issue: Difficulty Establishing a Circadian Rhythm

It's common for infants to mix up night and day when they are first born, sleeping while the sun is up but becoming active come nightfall. While it may be easy to think, "well, hey, any sleep is good sleep!" Unfortunately, this can make it much more challenging to establish a healthy rhythm later. Not only that, but most parents sleep during the night, so being up all night and all day with your baby can take a toll on your physical and mental health.

How to Solve This Issue: While your baby will most likely grow out of this pattern of sleeping all day and partying all night, there are ways to fix this rhythm early. Make sure that your baby associates sunlight with wakefulness. This can be done by either introducing natural light into their room in the morning or moving them to a sunlit room shortly after they wake. You also want to reduce your baby's blue light exposure during the day. For example, if you watch TV with your baby in the room, make sure to turn it off before the sun goes down.

Issue: Restlessness After Night Feedings

Your baby will frequently wake up during the first three months to feed, filling their bellies one, two, and even three times a night to get the nutrients they need. For some babies, this stimulation can cause them to struggle when trying to go back to bed. This problem only worsens as the night gets on, as a baby who has just fallen back asleep and quickly wakes up again to eat will undoubtedly be fussier.

How to Solve This Issue: All babies are unique, and your infant may be feeding too often at night. Overfeeding can often cause sleeplessness, and if the time between these feedings is shorter due to being awake, your baby won't get the rest it needs. The solution is to feed them less often, but you'll want to visit your paediatrician to discuss this before changing their feeding schedule. If they approve, you will likely increase their daytime feedings and stretch out the time between night-time feedings so they can get proper rest.

Sleep Problems in Stage 2: 3-6 Months

Issue: Sleep Regression

It's possible for the first few months of your baby's sleep to seem to progress and improve, only for a sudden drop to occur around the 3-4 month mark. This is called sleep regression, and it may happen every few months. During sleep regression, the times your baby used to get tired changes dramatically, and they will be far more awake or active at inconvenient times. Your baby may even appear to be fighting the urge to sleep and will wake up more often once they drift off.

How to Solve This Issue: While it may seem counterintuitive, sticking to the same routine that your baby is resisting is often the best way to break through sleep regression. Whatever your usual night-time ritual is, whether that be a pre-bed feed, nightly bath, storytime, or gentle lullabies, it should be kept in place. You can also supplement the time your baby loses during night-time regression occurrences by increasing the number of naps they have during the day. Remember, sleep regression is a temporary phenomenon. Push through, and your baby will be back on their regular sleep schedule in a few days or weeks.

Issue: Changes in Nap Schedule

Babies will progressively nap less throughout their first year of life, and this usually translates to longer stretches of sleep during the night. On the other hand, if your baby is napping less but showing signs that they are tired or struggling to sleep at night, they may need to nap more to get the sleep they need.

How to Solve This Issue: You can encourage your baby to nap by going through a routine similar to the one you use at night. While mimicking your bedtime routine, this nap routine will be much shorter, but it should still be effective in letting your baby know it's time to rest. A good example would be if you have a decent bit of storytime before bed and read a short story before a nap. Eventually, this irregularity should correct itself, but in the meantime, it's important your baby naps as much as they need to.

Sleep Problems in Stage 3: 6-12 Months

Issue: Can't Get Back to Sleep on Their Own

Much like adults, babies may wake up during the night for no real reason at all. At this stage, they will usually drift back to sleep on their own, and learning how to do so is a necessary habit for them to develop as they age. On the other hand, If a baby between six and twelve months needs to be fed or rocked to sleep each time it wakes up, that may signal they are having a problem with their sleep patterns.

How to Solve This Issue: If your baby is having trouble falling asleep independently, you may want to do a bit of sleep training. This means establishing a good bedtime routine and noting what behaviour's usually encourage your baby to fall asleep quickly. You will want to place your baby in the spot where they typically sleep, giving them a way to self-soothe in case they wake up. A pacifier is a great example; if your baby wakes up, they will use the pacifier to soothe themselves instead of relying on you to get them settled.

Issue: Teething Pain Disrupting Sleep

Most babies will get their first tooth by the time they are six months old, and teething pain will persist while the rest of their teeth start to grow. You will see the signs of this pain throughout the day, with biting, fussing, drooling, and general irritability being the most common indicators. Teething pain can carry on into the night, waking your baby frequently and interrupting its sleep.

How to Solve This Issue: It will be tempting to pick up and hold your baby during these teething pain spells, but you should do your best to leave them be. Too much attention will make them focus on the teething pain by associating it with receiving attention. Instead, give your baby a teething ring, and give them a few gentle pats or shushes before leaving the room. Talk to your paediatrician about medication like baby aspirin if the problem persists.

Tips for Safe Sleeping

In addition to ensuring their sleep is as restful as possible, you'll want to ensure your infant is safe during both night and naptime.

There are a few guidelines you can follow to make sure their sleeping environment is the safest it can be, along with a few behaviour's you can take part in to reduce their risk of injury.

- Make sure your baby always sleeps on their back. You'll want to monitor your baby while it's sleeping until it gets into this habit, as many babies will naturally try to sleep on their stomachs.
- Keep the room at an appropriate level of darkness and within the optimal temperature range. This is usually between 68 and 72 degrees Fahrenheit, though some babies may prefer a cooler temperature.
- Use a cradle or crib that meets all safety guidelines, and ensure it has been correctly assembled. If possible, purchase your crib new; that way, you won't have to worry whether it has any pieces that have worn down or become compromised.
- Dress your baby in a fitted onesie, and make sure their crib is clear of all pillows, toys, and blankets before they sleep.
- Find a firm and flat mattress for their crib with a tight-fitting sheet, and keep the crib in the same room where you sleep for the first six months.
- Avoid bed-sharing with your infant. The safest place for your infant to sleep is in their crib, and bed-sharing can increase their risk of injury or death. If you do bed share, make sure that your bed is set to the same conditions as your baby's crib. That means a firm mattress, fitted sheet, and no blankets, pillows, or toys that could suffocate the baby.

From Sleep to Sass: Let's Talk About Your Baby's Emotions

Now that we've covered the different sleep stages your infant will go through in the first year and their associated issues, let's move on to your baby's ability to regulate their emotions. Learning self-control and developing emotional intelligence are important building blocks in your infant's growth, and starting early is always better. In our next chapter, we'll discuss what self-regulation is, why it's important, and how you can help your baby develop it in the first twelve months of their life.

Dad Hacks From Chapter 4

Sleep Hack #1: Establish a Bedtime Routine. Whether you read your children's stories, bath them, or sing them songs, create an activity that signals to your infant's brain that it's almost time to sleep.

Sleep Hack #2: Use the Power of Natural Sunlight. Exposing your infant to sunlight first thing in the morning will help them develop their circadian rhythms sooner, leading to better sleep patterns at the early stages of development.

Sleep Hack #3: Watch for the Sleep Deficiency Signals. If your baby is constantly yawning, fluttering their eyelids, losing interest in activities that usually stimulate them, tightening their fists, or crying more frequently, they may be sleep deprived. Identify these signs early to correct the problem and get them back into a healthy sleep pattern.

Sleep Hack #4: Make Sure Your Baby Sleeps On Its Back. One of the easiest ways to ensure your child's safety while they sleep is to make sure they sleep on their back. Watch your baby closely during their sleep, and turn them over whenever they start to shift to their stomach. Babies prefer stomach sleeping, but through consistent sleep training, they will learn to associate back positioning with bedtime.

Sleep Hack #5: Find a Comfort Item. A safe bedtime comfort item can help your baby learn to fall asleep independently and

---

reduce the amount you need to tend to them at night. This shouldn't be a toy or blanket, as that could cause the baby to suffocate. Instead, use an item like a pacifier designed to go in a baby's mouth without harming them.

Chapter 5

How to Teach Your Baby to Develop Self-Regulation

We've all had it happen: you are eating at a restaurant, sitting at a local sports game, or walking through the mall, and no matter what you do, your baby just won't stop crying. Maybe they're upset that the restaurant doesn't have a good wine selection, perhaps they placed a large bet on the game, and their team is losing, or maybe the mall Santa that year is a bit weird and smells like old bread. Whatever the reason, it can be frustrating when your baby won't calm down. The cause for their distress is simple; they have yet to develop the ability to self-regulate their emotions.

In truth, it's very reasonable that a baby would have difficulty with self-regulation, or the ability to control one's emotions rather than act on impulse. But the sooner your baby learns this skill, the better; developing self-regulation early can help your baby later in several ways, including:

- *Learning in School:* A child that is screaming and crying in school may be removed from a classroom, causing them to fall behind in their education and miss important lessons. It's also more challenging to take in information if your emotions are getting the better of you; a well-behaved child is more likely to focus and soak up everything that school has to offer, setting them up for success as they advance in their educational career.

- *Making Friends:* No one wants to invite a mini-Godzilla to their birthday party, and an out-of-control child will face an uphill battle to find willing playmates. Socializing and making friends are essential foundational events in a baby's life, but without self-regulation, it's unlikely other children will want to play or converse with your child. By learning to take turns in games, share their toys with other children, and express their emotions in a healthy and measured manner, your baby will be more likely to form strong connections and create lasting friendships.

- *Behaving Themselves Socially:* Regulating emotions can keep a person from acting in socially inappropriate ways. For example, if your child is screaming and crying in a store, you will likely feel embarrassed and may even be asked to leave. A child without emotional self-regulation may also participate in behaviour's that could damage property or injure themselves and others. If a child is mad and doesn't know how to handle it, they may lash out physically or destroy the things around them. Teaching your child to control their emotions early can save them from the consequences of these types of actions.

- *Becoming Independent:* Developing self-regulation means that your child will understand how to calmly assess different situations and make rational, appropriate decisions on how to act. This means they will be coming to you less for guidance, which will become incredibly important later on in their lives. While a baby is naturally very dependent on their parents, emotional self-regulation is the first step in moving towards the eventual self-reliance they will have to develop.

Several different activities and events can send a baby into a negative emotional state, and without self-regulation, they will have difficulty self-soothing and becoming calm. These activities can be almost anything, including hunger between meals, a dirty diaper, unfamiliar guests, loud noises, or a strange new environment. As your child grows, they will need to learn to adapt and adjust to new experiences without giving in to their emotions or impulses. This is the basis for learning self-regulation, and while it may take years for your child to develop this skill fully, you'll want to start identifying and strengthening their ability to do so as soon as possible.

Let's start by discussing how self-regulation manifests in different stages of your baby's first year and how your infant will slowly develop these skills over time. Look for the various signals that show what emotions your baby is dealing with; that way, you can adjust your soothing strategies and help bring that back into a calm, happy state.

Self-Regulation in the First Twelve Months

So what does self-regulation look like in children? Well, it varies from month to month. As your baby's brain develops, they will learn to process and express their emotions in different ways. Every child is unique, but if we are speaking in general terms, self-regulation usually involves:

- The ability to focus on a task
- How well your baby can switch from one task to the next
- The ability to control impulses
- Not overreacting to emotions like anger, embarrassment, excitement, and frustration

- Behaving with other children and adults

In the early stages of your infant's life, it won't be easy to discern whether certain aspects of this self-regulation are happening. As your baby becomes more mobile and expressive, you should be able to see how far along their self-regulation skills have advanced.

Self-Regulation Signs: *Months 0-3*

When your baby is a newborn, it's not easy to quantify how much emotional regulation is taking place. That being said, there are a few common signs to watch for:

Sign #1: Attention Span and Spotlight

During the first three months of its life, your baby will display its level of emotional regulation largely by how it focuses on items of interest. Most infants at this stage have a very "sticky" attention spotlight; this means that if they begin to focus on something, it will be difficult to change their focus to something else. If your baby can focus on a single item of interest and has no difficulty switching to and concentrating on another item, that likely means they already have some modicum of self-regulation abilities.

Sign #2: Alertness and Sleep-Wake Patterns

One sign of poor emotional self-regulation is how your baby deals with the sleeping and waking parts of their day. The more erratic a baby's sleep schedule, the more likely they will have a tough time controlling their emotions. Now, this is completely understandable at this stage of infancy. Babies initially have erratic sleep patterns, and the subsequent trouble with self-regulation is a byproduct. However, the more you can do to regulate their sleep patterns, the more they will be able to control their emotions. Refer to Chapter 4 for ways to help your baby get the best sleep possible.

Sign #3: Behaviour Governed by Reflex and Sensation

A baby's behaviour in the first three months of their life will primarily be controlled by their reflexes and how they respond to different sensations. So if your baby feels the sensation of hunger, it will likely begin to cry. If your baby feels tired, it will also start to cry. Basically, many different sensations will activate their reflex to cry, as they don't yet possess the self-regulation tools to deal with these feelings.

Self-Regulation Signs: *Months 3-6*

During months three to six, your baby will develop stronger self-regulation skills, especially if they get proper sleep and behavioural encouragement. There are a few signs to look for that can help you determine their self-regulation in this stage.

Sign #1: Intentional Behaviours

One sign of increased emotional regulation you will see during this stage is more intentional behaviour's. Your baby will start to move not just around but towards particular objects. They will also reach out and grasp things that they are focusing on. The more they engage in these behaviour's, the more they develop their self-regulation abilities. You can facilitate this by giving them the freedom to move about as they like or bring objects they are focusing on close so they can grab them.

Sign #2: Increased Alertness Time

Your baby's self-regulation will increase along with their alertness time, which can manifest in a few different ways:

- *Active State:* This form of alertness involves frequent movement and changing focus, along with your baby making small audible sounds. These movements will usually follow a certain rhythm and occur in small bursts. This may be your baby simply responding to a stimulus, but it can also be a warning sign that they may soon become fussy.

- *Quiet State:* Another alertness stage involves our baby quieting down but still engaging and looking for physical interaction. Your baby may touch your face or hands and focus on the sound of your voice. There is much less movement during this stage as your baby focuses on seeing and hearing. The quiet state is the ideal precursor to drowsiness and sleep, as it symbolizes they are entering a more calm and relaxed state of mind.

- *Crying State:* Crying is a baby's reflexive response to various emotions, sensations, and stimuli, usually when they feel some type of discomfort. This usually comes in the form of hunger or tiredness. A baby in a crying state will move more aggressively, shifting their arms and legs and contouring their face into an unpleasant expression. The crying state can usually be helped by soothing your baby and identifying what issue is causing their distress.

- *Drowsy State:* Before each instance of sleep, your baby will almost always enter a state of least alertness, the drowsy state. During this time, your baby will move very little but still make certain facial expressions like smiling or frowning. They will struggle to remain focused on much of anything, with their eyes glazing and eyelids drooping. If you see your baby enter this state, it's best to move them to their designated sleeping area so they can rest.

Sign #3: More Regulated Sleep Patterns

The times your baby isn't alert, whether it be when they are asleep at night or during a nap, become far more regulated as you enter months three through six. If they remain chaotic, that will almost always reduce your baby's ability to self-regulate their emotions. If your baby is struggling to establish a solid circadian rhythm or sleep pattern, you'll want to take steps to correct it as soon as possible. Again, refer to chapter 4 for tips on how to help your baby sleep properly.

Self-Regulation Signs: *Months 6-12*

During the last six months of your baby's first year, their ability to self-regulate will expand exponentially. This will show in their ability to maintain their attention, their mannerisms, and how they perceive patterns.

Sign #1: Flexible Attention Adjustment

At this point, a good marker for your baby's self-regulation abilities is whether they can shift their attention. If a baby is flexible in how they move their focus from different people and objects to new areas of interest, that means they are keeping their emotions in check. Your baby may be unable to do this all the time, and this skill won't become fully established for the next few years. But the ability to focus on an object for a few seconds and then switch to another is an excellent sign for their emotional development.

Sign #2: Pattern Recognition

Around this stage, your baby will begin to recognize simple, repetitive patterns. These are almost always very simple, like stripes of colours, certain numbers, basic images, and shapes. Playing with toys like blocks and putting them into a recognizable pattern is a good way to build this pattern recognition skill. Recognizing patterns can also increase your baby's reasoning ability, leading to better emotional regulation later in life.

Sign #3: Movement and Mannerisms

The development of certain regulation systems will also take place during this stage, with your baby moving and acting in ways to react calmly to different sensations. For example, if your baby is feeling overstimulated and has learned to recognize when it's occurring, they will turn their head away from you (or the source of stimulation.) At the same time, babies may begin to suck their thumbs in response to stressful events. This shows they recognize when something is overwhelming them and are self-soothing to regulate their emotions.

Tips to Improve Your Baby's Self-Regulation

Two basic ways to improve your baby's self-regulation are to teach them self-control and increase their self-confidence. Here are a couple of tips you can use to do so.

Tips for Increasing Self-Control

- *Lead by Example:* While this will become more helpful later once your baby can recognize behavioural patterns, you'll want to lead by example when it comes to self-control. Don't lose your cool in front of the baby, and manage your own anger when situations become frustrating.
- *Show Them How to Act in Public:* Babies cry in public; it's an unavoidable fact of life. Whether this happens in a restaurant, grocery store, movie theatre, church, or anywhere else, make sure not to overreact. Calmly soothe your baby, as this will teach them that this isn't the place to lose control of their emotions. You can also take them outside to remove them from the negative stimuli that may be causing their emotional reaction.

- *Establish a Routine:* Babies are more likely to learn self-control if they find comfort in a regular routine. Meals, baths, bedtime and naptime, all of these regular daily events should follow a similar path each and every day—for example, your routine at bedtime. If you feed your baby, read them a story, and then tuck them in, make sure to do this sequence of events in the same way, every night.

Tips for Increasing Self-Confidence

- *Comfort Your Baby:* Your baby will feel much more confident if it can feel safe in a calm and comforting environment. In infants, self-control mostly depends on how they self-soothe; when your baby is upset, it needs to learn how to calm itself down in case you aren't around. Their sleeping environment is an excellent example of this. Having a dark enough room to sleep in but still with soft lighting sources, as well as a comfortable crib, can help a baby calm itself down when it wakes up at night.
- *Respond to Your Baby's Needs:* Your baby will signal when it's having difficulty with certain stimuli or emotions, and you'll want to recognize these signs and respond accordingly. Whether your baby is crying, giving you a certain facial expression, or gesturing in a particular way, observe what caused this reaction and adjust your behaviour accordingly.
- *Use Positive Reinforcement:* Positive reinforcement is a great way to help your baby discern which actions are appropriate and which aren't, which can boost their self-confidence. This positive reinforcement can take many forms, including:

- A gentle high five
- Smiling
- Clapping
- A thumbs-up
- Cheering
- Giving them their favourite toy
- Telling them, they are a cool little fella or gal (or a less goofy compliment)
- Patting them on the back

Any of these actions function as effective behavioural modification and serve to encourage prosocial behaviour's. These behaviour's include following directions, eating a meal without fuss, sharing their toys with playmates, and refraining from hurting themselves, property, or others.

Making Your Baby Feel At Ease: Tune in to Their Temperament

One of the best ways to determine how your baby is dealing with their emotions is to become familiar with their temperament. Temperament is how people of any age deal with the world around them; this means overcoming challenges, managing feelings, and acting on or ignoring impulses.

There are three major components to your baby's temperament:

1. *Mood*

While it can be easy to determine an adult's mood because of their ability to vocalize their feelings, it can be much more difficult to accurately assess how a baby is feeling. Try to observe your baby's facial expressions, movements, and noises during various activities. An upset baby will usually screw up their face as though they ate something sour, balling their fists and crying to let you know they are displeased. These are more general traits, as every infant is unique; identify your baby's good and bad mood signs, then find ways to comfort them and lift their spirits.

2. *Adaptability*

Another foundational component of your baby's temperament is their ability to adapt to new situations. Learn your baby's strengths, what they excel at, and the activities they tend to struggle with. Maybe your baby is very good at sleeping in an unfamiliar location, like if you take them with you on vacation, but less adept at trying new foods. Learning their personality and what obstacles they are better suited to overcome can be incredibly helpful. You'll want to put your baby in situations they are more comfortable in on lousy mood days, then try to challenge them and get them outside of their box on their good mood days. Showing your baby how to adapt and be flexible will be very helpful later on in their lives, though it's a skill that often takes several years to internalize.

3. *Intensity*

Just as important as what situations elicit a reaction from your child is how intensely they react. When your baby is presented with a situation or sensation they don't like, do they make a face or burst out into loud sobs? If your child doesn't like a person or object, do they simply turn away or lash out physically? The intensity of your child's reactions is a very telling sign of their temperament; if they overreact to everyday situations, that's a good sign they'll need some behavioural training to improve their self-regulation.

71

Self-Regulation is Important, But Only One Part of the Equation

Starting early is key when helping your baby develop self-regulation, self-control, and self-confidence, but there are only some of the puzzle pieces that make up their minds. Your baby's mental state and emotional well-being are a complicated tapestry that you will need to assess and assist throughout their first year of life. In our next chapter, we'll look at how you can strengthen their emotional and mental health and the best ways to bond properly with your baby.

Dad Hacks From Chapter 5

Self-Regulation Hack #1: Provide Your Baby With Different Sensory Activities. It will be much easier to recognize your baby's emotional state and level of self-regulation if they can express themselves. By providing them with various sensory activities, you can expand the areas of their brain that allow them to make facial expressions and eventually vocalize their thoughts. A play gym is one great tool which gives infants various toys to play with to strengthen their hand-eye coordination and the muscles around the eyes. Another good sensory activity is reading to them, which stimulates the language centre in their brain.

Self-Regulation Hack #2: Track Your Child's Behaviour in a Journal. Watch your baby closely while it participates in various activities and see how it reacts to certain stimuli. Does your baby get easily frustrated? Do they play well with others and share their toys? Does your baby tend to focus on a given object of interest, and how easily can they adjust their focus? Take notes about your baby's reactions, and see how they change over time. Hopefully,

---

your baby begins to show signs they are developing their self-regulation skills; if not, that can indicate you should do more focused behavioural training.

Self-Regulation Hack #3: Don't Be Afraid to Intervene. It's easy to worry that by intervening when your baby is upset, you could make their mood even worse. But the best thing to do when your baby reacts strongly to a sensation or emotion is to actively engage with them and try to improve their mood. Soothe your baby when they are crying, or give them a toy or object that comforts them. If they are in an overstimulating setting, like a movie theatre, take them outside until they have calmed down.

Self-Regulation Hack #4: Organize Play Dates for Your Baby. One of the most significant advantages of proper self-regulation is behaving in social situations. Without learning self-control, your baby could grow up to be a person who does not treat others well and therefore loses out on the chance to socialize with their peers properly. Organize play dates for your baby early, and watch how they interact with others. Make sure to use positive reinforcement when your baby is kind and caring to other children; at the same time, let them know when their behaviour is inappropriate. Over time, your baby will learn the correct way to act in social situations, setting them up to make friends and meaningful connections as they grow.

Self-Regulation Hack #5: Keep their Comfort Item Close. It may seem like a crutch, but it's not always possible to calm your child down with shushing and back rubs alone. At this point, you've likely identified a comfort item that your baby has fixated on. This may be a specific pacifier, toy, stuffed animal, or any other object that brings your baby comfort. Make sure this item is packed for any trip you take, even if it's just to the store or local park. Leaving your baby in an emotionally heightened state of crying or agitation isn't good for them. You'll want every tool available to you to help soothe their emotions quickly.

Chapter 6

How to Help Your Baby Develop Their Mental and Emotional Health

Caring for your baby's mental and emotional health can seem like an impossible task at times, mainly because your baby can't yet vocalize its feelings. Taking a self-care day or helping out a loved one can be as simple as drawing a calming bath with a glass of wine or taking your partner on a romantic vacation. While we all wish we could give our child a warm glass of formula or a trip to the baby Bahamas to help them recharge, the fact is that your baby will need careful guidance to grow its mental faculties. Here are some tips to help develop your infant's mental health as they grow throughout their first year.

Mental Health Tips for Each Developmental Stage in Year One

First Development Stage: Month 1-3

From the time you first get home from the hospital through the next few months, you will begin to learn about your baby's personality and attune to their feelings. I remember our first child developing their baby talk early on, and I would always light up when I heard their happy squeaking. At the same time, it was easy to recognize when our baby wasn't having a good day; their signature pout would almost always be followed by a torrent of tears and frowns. There are a couple of ways you can help your baby in those first six months when you see an impending tantrum train coming down the tracks.

Tip #1: *Engage All Their Senses*

Allowing your baby to touch, feel, hear and move about freely is all important to align their physical and mental feelings. When they are first born, your child will likely not understand the sensations of movement and touch. If you give them freedom of movement, they will slowly learn to control how they interact with the world. Make sure you have a lot of skin-to-skin contact with them as well; this can comfort your baby as it interacts with the world, making them feel more secure and confident in their exploration.

Tip #2: *Soft Tones, Smiles, and Baby Talk Time*

Positive reinforcement and communication are foundational to strengthening your baby's mental health. Much like with our child's happy squeaks, your baby will develop their own pre-language way of communicating with you. Encourage this by baby-talking back, using soft tones and smiling while you speak. Make sure to use real words with your infant, as they will start to emulate your speech and expand the language centers of their brain. You can also change the tone and volume of your voice to see how your baby reacts to changes in speech, gauging how their facial expressions and vocalizations change as your behavior shifts.

Tip #3: *Soothe and Stimulate*

Use toys like a rattle or bell to pull your baby's focus and help them move around. Moving a shiny toy in front of them up and down can help them develop their neck and shoulder muscles. If your baby becomes overstimulated, and it looks like the dark cloud of a crying storm is moving in, soothe your baby by rubbing them gently on the back. If your baby does tip over into a tantrum, pick them up and cuddle them; this will almost always help them calm down and get back to smiling and playing.

Second Development Stage: Month 3-6

At this point, your baby will start to develop better vision, and many objects will begin to take shape in their mind. By month three, it's like they've found little baby glasses they can put on, giving them more confidence and an increased desire to explore. Depending on your baby's temperament, they will still be very attached to you and your partner. Our second child was particularly devoted to their mom, and I could only get their attention by bribing them with a new rattle or shiny set of keys. Be careful with this toy bribery method though; if your baby is anything like mine was, they'll try to eat your car keys the second you turn your back!

Here are some mental health tips for months 3-6.

Tip #1: *Show Them a Variety of Photos*

At this point, your baby will start to identify shapes and colors, so you should show them a wide variety of pictures. While it may be tempting to show them those vacation pictures no one else seems interested in, it's much better to have them look at things, places, and people they may interact with in the outside world. Observe how your baby interacts with each picture, and say the name of everything they see to help establish a connection in their mind. An excellent place to start is with animals; you may even find out your baby's favorite animal before their first word! Our first child loved dolphins and would smile endlessly, looking at photos of them diving in and out of the water, leading to many future trips to the aquarium.

Tip #2: *Mirror Your Baby's Sounds and Play Games With Them*

Smile, laugh, and try to make the same faces or gestures your baby does as a way to pull their focus. This gets them to develop their facial recognition skills and helps keep them in a good mood. You can also play little games, like the classic "peek-a-boo". Hide your face behind your hands, peeking through your fingers until your baby changes their expression. Then remove your hands and exclaim (with a big smile, of course) and watch them laugh and squeal.

Tip #3: *Encourage Your Baby to Follow and Touch Safe Objects*

You'll also want to show your baby how to focus on particular objects and learn what things are safe to touch. Something like a colorful cup is a good one to start with; simply move the cup in front of their face until their eyes are clearly following it. Move up, down, left, right, then move it within their grip range. You want them to reach out and touch it, learning that it's safe to do so. Make sure it's made of a nonbreakable material though; I remember our baby grabbing my favorite mug off the table and dropping it to the floor. We were both crying that day!

Third Development Stage: Month 6-12

At six months old, your baby's exploration will reach new heights as they begin to crawl around your home. This can be both a blessing and a curse; nothing is more stressful than looking at your phone for a moment, only to look up and see that your baby has vanished into thin air. I suggested to my partner we put a bell on our child to keep track of them, but this idea was shot down. Instead, make sure you keep a close eye on them as they learn locomotion and continue finding ways to strengthen their mental and emotional health. Here are some tips for months 6-12.

Tip #1: *Words, Words, Words*

At this point, you should be saying as many words as possible to your baby, particularly their name. Your baby will learn to recognize their name and turn their head to whoever is saying it, which becomes particularly helpful when they start to crawl. You'll also want to point to places and objects, helping them associate the word with its meaning. Make sure not to speak too loudly, as this can scare them or create negative associations with whatever they interact with. Instead, smile and speak in gentle tones, putting your baby at ease and allowing them to learn in a comforting environment.

Tip #2: *Provide Your Baby With Safe, Colorful Objects*

Your baby will naturally reach out, grab, and fiddle about with anything within arm's reach, so make sure to provide safe things for them to do so with. Our first baby was particularly fond of wooden spoons, which they would bang like drumsticks onto their high chair. As long as the object is not breakable, any wooden or plastic thing should work perfectly fine. You can also give your baby simple puzzles or picture books to look at; anything that will stimulate their brain. Make sure the puzzle pieces aren't too small, or your baby may mistake them for a flavorless choking hazard to munch on.

Tip #3: *Connect Sounds to Gestures*

As your baby's brain develops, it will start to draw connections between movements and vocal expressions. Encourage this by showing the baby common expressions, like "good-bye." As someone leaves your home, wave to them while saying "bye" and then move your baby's hand. You can also do this when someone arrives, saying hello and placing your baby's hand up. This will teach them to imitate these movements and recognize the correct reactions in social situations.

How to Bond With Your Baby

While bonding with a new friend or coworker is as simple as getting a beer together, finding a mutual interest or type of music, bonding with your baby is very different. For one, your baby probably doesn't have the same taste in music (even if the Wiggles do have a couple of pretty good songs.) Bonding with a baby is more about the natural attachment, and unconditional love parents and children develop for one another throughout the first stages of life.

This process can take a few weeks to several months as the mutual love grows gradually. It's important not to panic if you don't feel that love blossoms instantly, as these emotions can take time to kick in. Pregnancy and childbirth are stressful, as is being a parent. I didn't get this bond for several months after our first child was born; believe me, I was freaking out. But there are ways to encourage that strong, loving feeling to grow; let's talk about a few ways to help develop an emotional bond with your baby.

6 Ways to Bond With Your Baby

1. Big Smiles, Happy Talks

Studies have shown that babies can recognize smiles from an early age, and this ability only gets stronger as their eyesight improves with age. The same goes for happy speech, and while they don't yet have the ability to respond verbally, your baby will bond with you simply by smiling back and listening to you talk. They also learn the power of smiling early on, and by mirroring this behaviour back to them, you encourage them to associate smiling with feelings of happiness.

2. Funny Faces

It may seem goofy, but making funny faces to entertain your child actually enhances their ability to bond with you. Your baby will imitate the faces you make and start to recognize whether a facial expression means someone is happy or sad. As your baby learns your emotions and you learn theirs, the bond between you will strengthen. Don't be afraid to make the silliest faces possible with your child; just because it's a bit childish doesn't mean it's not helpful (and fun!)

3. Karaoke Often

Karaoke isn't just for embarrassing yourself in front of your coworkers on a Friday night; it's also great for entertaining your baby. Singing helps your baby identify your distinct voice and can even be used to establish a routine for your child's day. If you sing a song every night before bedtime, you may see your baby start to get tired before they even get to their crib. The songs don't have to be nursery rhymes either; belt out your favorite pop songs, musical numbers, or anything else. As long as you look happy and your baby smiles, your bond is stronger.

4. Dance the Day Away

In the same vein as singing, dancing is an excellent way to show your baby positive emotions and how to move around freely. It also helps relieve stress and release those feel-good hormones in your body, which can directly affect your (and your baby's) mood. Dance while your child is watching, or pick them up and carefully have them join you. This can be a soothing method when your baby is upset or tired, getting them moving and taking their mind off their discomfort.

5. Skin to Skin Contact

Skin to skin contact has been proven to relax and calm both the parent and child, lowering your baby's heart rate and giving their breathing a healthier rhythm. It can also regulate their temperature, stimulate their digestion, and interest them more in feeding. Holding your baby to your skin is an excellent bonding technique and should be done frequently, starting shortly after their birth. Simply hold contact for 30 minutes at a time in a calm and relaxed environment to avoid overstimulating your baby. In no time, you will feel a connection with your child, and they will likewise associate you with love, safety, and a feeling of calm.

6. One on One Time

Part of getting your baby to bond with you is separating yourself from other people they interact with. While many family and friends will want to visit soon after the birth, you and your partner should spend plenty of one on one time with the baby. Your child needs to become comfortable with your touch, voice, and presence; this accelerates the bonding process and helps them understand that you are their primary protector and provider.

Bonding With the Help of Baby Talk

While seemingly nonsensical, baby talk is one of the best bonding techniques you can utilize. Studies have shown that engaging a baby in normal conversation activates different sections of its brain, but baby talk causes those same parts to light up dramatically. Your baby's brain is developing rapidly in its first few years of life, forming connections and processing information that will help it learn and think. If you want to help these synapses grow quickly and bond with your baby simultaneously, you'll need to act just a little bit silly.

The best baby talk teacher you'll have is...well, your baby. They will engage you with those classic goo's and gah's, and you can emulate them. Just make sure not to interrupt your baby while they are talking. Pretending your baby is like a friend telling you a story you can't follow; nod your head politely, maintain eye contact, and let them know you are listening. Once there is a break in the conversation, respond with a mixture of similar noises and grown-up talk. All of this trains your baby's brain to identify the call-and-response nature of conversation, which will be incredibly helpful as they develop their speaking ability.

How you talk with your baby will also change over the first year. Let's break down the different stages of development and how you should engage in baby talk for each.

Month 1-3

Your infant's communication will be very limited at this stage and will usually consist of gurgles, goo's, coohs, and a baby's favorite: crying. This is accompanied by movement and smiles; observe how your baby moves and reacts to your speech, and adjust your tone and volume to elicit a happy response. For the first three months, you'll want to:

- Keep it simple. Talk, sing, and babble like your baby would, keeping the tone light and happy.
- Narrate what you are doing. While your baby won't quite be able to process it yet, saying what is happening will help them form the foundational connections between speech and action.
- After a few months, your baby will be able to make some sounds resembling words. Mimic them when they do this, and say some words that include those vowel sounds. For example, if they start saying "ah", say "aeroplane."

- Start to get them in the rhythm of conversation. Let them talk, and then talk back to them when they stop.

Month 3-6

At this point, your baby will start to get the hang of copying certain sounds and even parts of words. It's even possible that they learn to control the volume of their voice, raising it if you get further away and lowering it as you get close. To encourage this development, you'll want to:

- Help them finish words that they seem to be attempting to vocalize. This is less abstract than the "aeroplane" example from the first stage; if a baby is pointing towards their bottle and saying "bah", you can say "bottle" and hand it to them.
- Ask your baby questions during a conversation, and start to establish a narrative flow. For example, show them a toy, like their favorite rattle or pacifier. Ask them, "do you want your rattle?" and wait for them to respond positively. Wait until they vocalize their want in some manner, then hand them the rattle.
- Reading is also important; at this point, you should read aloud from books to your child daily. This helps expose them to a much larger set of words, and if the books have pictures, it helps them form associations between those words and their meanings.

Month 6-12

In the later part of the first year, your baby may begin to say the beginnings or endings of words, and it's even possible they will say their first complete word. You should be encouraging this at every step of the way by doing things like:

- Naming everything that they point to or come in contact with. If your child is about to get in the car, say, "we are getting in the car." If your baby is pointing to their food, tell them the name or the utensils you use to feed them.
- Try to be as positive as possible when talking with your baby. If they are fussing, you don't want to say, "stop doing that" you want to say, "it's time to sit still." You can also help them express their feelings by saying them out loud. For example, if they seem giddy or happy, you can say, "whose happy?" and smile back at them.
- Be careful what words you say at this point, as your baby will begin to imitate them fully. This is why curse words should be kept to a minimum (though this becomes more important later on as your child develops their speech abilities fully.) I made the mistake of exclaiming loudly once when I stubbed my toe, and one of our children made that their favorite word for the next month.

Your Relationship With Your Baby is Stronger, But What About With Your Partner?

Bonding with your baby is vital to providing them with the feelings of comfort they need to grow. But the early stages of childhood can be a very straining time for you and your partner, with many parents allowing their romantic relationship to fall by the wayside. In our next chapter, we'll talk about the common challenges and changes that may occur in your relationship and the different ways to solve these new problems.

Dad Hacks From Chapter 6

Mental Health Hack #1: Mirroring is Key. Imitation is the sincerest form of flattery, and your baby will be copying your every move. Make sure to return the favor and help reinforce associations between movements and words.

Mental Health Hack #2: Skin to Skin Contact Helps Bonding. As one of the strongest tools in your bond-building strategy, skin to skin contact can quickly create a long-lasting emotional connection between you and your baby. Not only that, but it can also relieve stress, lower your baby's heart rate, and help bring their breathing under control.

Mental Health Hack #3: Don't Overstimulate. While you want to show your baby a wide variety of photos and help them understand the world around them, it's important not to overstimulate. If your baby begins to get fussy or cry while you teach, take a break to soothe them. A couple of shushes, gentle singing, and a back rub can bring your baby back to calm so they can get back to learning efficiently.

Mental Health Hack #4: Help Your Baby Finish Words. As your baby's language centers develop, they will start to vocalize noises that almost sound like full words. Help them finish these words, sounding out each syllable so they can begin to form those associations in their brains.

Mental Health Hack #5: Identify Everything Around You. Especially important in the latter half of the first year, you'll want to teach your baby the name of every object, person, and place they interact with. If you make them a mini-Italian dinner, make sure to say, "this is spaghetti." If your sister comes over to visit, let them know, "this is your auntie." These behaviors will make it that much easier once they start to speak and help them understand not only the names of things but the meaning behind those names.

Chapter 7

How to Keep Your Relationship Going Strong, Even After Having a Baby

While having a baby can be one of life's most beautiful and rewarding experiences, it is also difficult, stressful, and exhausting. I'm ashamed to admit it, but my partner and I had our fair share of fights during the first year, often about nothing. I remember waking up late at night, thinking there was an emergency with the baby. Instead, I was confronted with an empty jar of peanut butter, my partner shaking it and whisper-yelling in an accusatory tone. "You ate every last BITE!" she said through gritted teeth, knowing she couldn't wake the baby. In my half-asleep daze, I started laughing; thankfully, so did she. But it goes to show you how stressful sleepless nights can get and how even the silliest thing can set one of you off.

It's strange to go from the two-person unit of a couple to a complete family, and the adjustment period isn't easy. You spend your whole life forming this idea of yourself in your head; then you tack on more years forging a relationship with someone. Now, suddenly, there is this tiny little person who pops into your life. It's a beautiful thing and one of the most significant events you can experience in your life, but it also dumps a myriad of new issues onto your plate. Fortunately, all obstacles can be overcome, and many couples find that they are much stronger for the struggle once they get through to the other side. Let's look at a few relationship changes you can expect after your first baby is born and how to deal with them.

Issue #1: Restructuring Your Lives

Babies are vulnerable and heavily dependent beings, requiring constant attention and care during the first months (and years) of their life. Before your infant is born, even during the pregnancy months, you and your partner will still have a lot of agency as individuals. You may go out, see friends, go on trips, sleep without disruption, and enjoy the freedom that comes without the responsibility of children. Once your kid is born, however, that will shift dramatically. Even if you think you are prepared, this significant change can still do a number on your romantic relationship.

Remember that weekly night out for dinner? You can kiss that goodbye (for a bit.) How about going on a run as a couple or sitting down to cuddle up for a movie? Sayonara. Your baby will need help with feeding, napping, diaper changes and will basically need to be monitored almost every second during the day. This loss of identity can be tough, and it's natural for couples to fight a bit as they feel the weight of that responsibility. My spouse's first stressful tug came with our weekly "old movie" night. We cherished that time, sitting down and picking some ancient black and white film to put on in the background as we inhaled popcorn. But something about those movies just stressed our first child, and we had to do away with the ritual for a while. Become comfortable with sacrifice, and realize that eventually, you'll be able to do most of these activities again.

Issue #2: Sleepless Nights and Weary Days

Sleep deprivation is a wild beast, a monster that, left unchecked, will tear at your sanity and the love you feel for your partner. Unfortunately, some level of sleeplessness is unavoidable during early parenthood. Make sure to look out for the signs of serious sleep deprivation, which include:

- Difficulty Thinking Clearly
- Bad Short-Term Memory
- Poor Decision making
- Lack of Energy
- Reduced Attention Span
- Severe Mood Swings

Sleep deprivation can also fill you with anxiety and make you irritable, something I struggled with. I'm someone who really can't survive without a solid 8 hours, so when I was averaging between 4 and none at all, I was indeed not my best self. Luckily, my spouse is genuinely kind and understanding (as long as you don't eat all of her peanut butter) and puts up with both the baby's temper tantrums and mine.

Issue #3: Feeling Frustrated and Helpless

I won't lie to you: the weight of having a living, breathing person depend on you for their protection and safety is terrifying. Even with all the advice and parenting books in the world, no one can truly prepare you for what it means to be responsible for someone else's life. It's understandable for you and your partner to feel helpless and frustrated with the overwhelming needs of a newborn. There will be times when the baby won't stop crying, can't get to sleep, or won't eat, and it may cause strife in your relationship.

As new problems crop up, remember that you are a team. Give each other breaks, try to research new issues as much as possible, and comfort one another. You may feel upset or sad now and then, especially as you come to understand just how much your baby will need from you. But over time, I promise, it will get easier.

Issue #4: Focusing All of Your Attention on the Baby

Yes, your baby should be the #1 priority in your life after they are born (and probably for the rest of your life as well.) But that doesn't mean that every single scrap and ounce of your attention should go towards your infant. Neglecting to acknowledge and tend to your spouse's needs can devastate your relationship. There will already be a lot of stressors, including the lack of sleep, increasing costs due to childcare, and the loss of free time. Amongst this, it's essential to try your best to remember that your partner is still your partner, and you need to stay connected with them.

If possible, call a family member or friend to see if they can watch the baby for a few hours—just enough time to get some lunch or dinner and get some alone time with your significant other. Remind them how beautiful they are and how much you care about them, and discuss future plans for trips and vacations. The first stages of parenthood can be challenging, and it may feel like it'll be overwhelming forever. Plan for the future and strengthen your relationship any time you can.

Issue #5: Communication Becomes Strained

Communication is vital when it comes to healthy relationships, and a massive life event will understandably shake up your ability to communicate with one another. What used to be sharing thoughts and feelings, regaling each other with stories about your day, and trading cute little inside jokes has become more akin to the communication of ants. When ants talk to each other, they basically just barf up chemicals that send very clear messages. One ant will barf to the other, "food that way", and the other ant will throw up ", okay." While this is great for helping a fellow insect find the picnic, it just doesn't work for human communication.

Just like ants, your conversation may become very one-note and transactional. "The baby is crying", "it's time to change their diaper", and "the baby is hungry"; all of these are examples of the clipped sentences you'll be exchanging in those first few months. As patience runs thin and responsibilities stack, discussions will become demands. Make sure to watch how you talk to your partner and try to make these demands more like requests.

Issue #6: Spontaneity Goes Out the Window

Before the baby, I remember one weekend I came home, and my partner presented me with a plane ticket. "We're going to the coast," she said, her eyes bright and sparkling with excitement. I was taken aback at first, unsure if she was joking, but as she pointed to an open suitcase, I too lit up with excitement. I still look at pictures of that weekend trip, cherishing the memories of sunsets, margaritas, and the sand beneath our feet. Unfortunately, spontaneous trips like this will likely evaporate as the baby arrives.

After your child is born, everything will need to be planned well in advance. Gone are the days of asking, "hey, want to go out for dinner tonight?" as that would require finding a babysitter, getting together a baby bag, and worrying all night about your child. This doesn't mean that you won't have fun, but it will be different. That doesn't mean you can't find ways to surprise your partner, and you should still try to find childcare and go out every once in a while. Just prepare yourself to say goodbye to the gallivanting that you may have once enjoyed as you transition into the responsibility of parenthood.

Issue #7: Your Partner May Suffer from Postpartum Depression

It's very possible that your significant other will experience some form of postpartum depression after birth; dads can get it too! You'll want to watch for the signs of postpartum depression, which include:

- *Lack of Motivation:* One of the early symptoms of postpartum depression is a lack of energy and motivation. If you notice your partner isn't showering, feeding themselves, or generally avoiding self-care, you'll want to talk to them about their feelings. This lack of motivation also extends to tasks relating to your baby. Mothers suffering from PPD may forget to feed or watch their children and will struggle to bond properly.
- *Avoidance:* Another symptom is avoidance of friends and family. If you see your partner ignoring calls, turning friends away at the door, or sequestering themselves when family comes over to see the baby, take these as major red flags. The cause of this avoidance is usually the fear or anxiety that they aren't a good parent, even though these thoughts are almost always unfounded.
- *Mood Swings:* Anger, sadness, anxiety, panic attacks: all of these can accompany postpartum depression. If you see your partner switching through emotions at a fast pace, struggling to sleep at night, or speaking about baby-related fears, check in with them.
- *Thoughts of Harm or Suicide:* This is a more advanced symptom and one of the most worrying. PPD sufferers can begin to have dark thoughts of suicide and, in some cases, even attempt to end their life. They can also have intrusive thoughts about harming the baby, which may be voiced jokingly at first. Recognize this sign for its severity and contact a medical professional immediately.

Don't hesitate to contact a doctor if you believe you or your partner is dealing with postpartum depression. They can help you with treatments to get you through this challenging time; the sooner you seek treatment, the better!

Issue #8: It'll Feel Like You Almost Never Have Sex

It can be a sensitive subject for some, but the issue of sex after having a baby is pretty significant. It's not easy to get in the mood with baby vomit on your shirt and the very unsexy scent of dirty diapers in the air. Even after the four to six weeks of abstinence doctors recommend after birth, you and your partner may have very little interest in sex. You'll start to feel less like lovers and more like roommates who have agreed to take care of a baby.

It's crucial to kindle that intimacy whenever you can. Sex is vital to a healthy romantic relationship and can help boost the confidence of both parties. Not only that, but it's a huge stress reliever, something you'll need during the challenging months following birth.

5 Tips to Keeping Your Relationship Strong Post-Baby

1.   See Things from Your Partner's Perspective

Amidst a crisis or in the middle of an argument, it can be hard to approach your spouse from a place of empathy. Tasks get forgotten, things get overlooked, and disagreements get heated. It's important to remember that this is hard on both of you before the voices get raised and the accusations start flying. Sure, a mom's and dad's experiences are different, but at the end of the day, you are in this together. Acknowledge what the other person is going through and try not to "keep score." It's not about who did what on any particular day, but the long game of parenting.

2. Schedule a Weekly Check-in

A good way to get ahead of problems and stay tuned in to how your partner is feeling is with weekly check-ins. My partner and I enacted this practice after a particularly painful week ending a terrible (and utterly useless) fight. I missed a few diapers, she woke the baby up from a nap, and several more minor gaffs culminated in us deciding we needed to make a change. So, we started sequestering our complaints into one weekly session on Sunday; that way, we didn't let our disagreements get in the way of caring for our baby. By the time Sunday rolled around, a lot of the heat of those angry moments had cooled, and we could talk about things more reasonably.

3. Avoid Criticism and Talk Efficiently

A key to effective communication is to avoid criticism whenever possible. Accusing someone of making a mistake, especially when stressed out, will automatically make them defensive. Be intentional with your statements and get right to the problem. Instead of "Can you please give the baby a bath for once?" say, "Honey, I'm so tired I can barely stand. Would you mind bathing the baby tonight?" Approach issues with a bit of tact, and you'll be surprised at how willing your significant other will be to help out.

4. Make Time For Each other

While there won't be time for big romantic getaways in the near future, making time for one another is about the little moments. Hold your partner's hand, tell them how much they mean to you, and spark a conversation about non-baby-related subjects. Remind your significant other that they have their own identity and stay intimate in any way you can. This also means bringing up things you miss, or need, as a partner. That could be a hug, some words of affirmation, or even that it's been a long time since you were physically intimate.

5. "Parent" Each Other

In the same way, you think and care about your infant; you have to care for one another. No, that doesn't mean you'll have to pick up your partner and burp them but instead, give your significant other the same breaks you would give your baby. When your infant starts to get frustrated, I doubt your reaction is to tell them angrily to calm down. Give your partner the benefit of the doubt and try your best to approach them with compassion during this stressful time.

How to Rekindle Your Sex Life After Childbirth

Having a physical connection is important, but passion can understandably slip from your relationship shortly after a baby is born. For several weeks after birth, abstaining from sex is an absolute necessity. Most doctors recommend women avoid sexual activity for four to six weeks, as they need time to heal. There is usually a postpartum check at this point where a doctor will give the go-ahead; even then, some couples find they aren't quite ready to get intimate.

My partner and I struggled with this for some time after baby #1. They didn't feel sexy after the pregnancy, and I didn't feel the urge due to lack of sleep exhaustion; the desire to get intimate wasn't there. I thought this wouldn't be a big deal at first, but then I felt a distance growing between us. Realizing a problem was brewing, I started researching ways to get that passion burning again. Here are a few ways I found to help relight the fire of love and possibly help you start making baby number 2!

Compassion Creates Passion

Sex is a two-way street, and it helps to be compassionate regarding your partner's physical needs. Women often feel overwhelmed after a baby is born and are likely to judge their spouses for their sexual

96

urges. Men, on the other hand, feel rejected and undesired. As these two forces meet and intimacy continues to fade, your relationship can fall into turmoil.

The key is to tap into that compassion and ask your partner about their sexual feelings. Be empathetic, listen to their side of the story, and share your own. By opening up communication and doing your best to understand what they are going through, you can bring back those feelings of closeness that inspired you to be intimate in the first place.

Small Gestures Make Big Impacts

I'm guilty of that old trope, the "grand romantic gesture." I made a bit of a gaff after our second child, in which I organized some time away only a few months after they were born. I was frustrated when my partner wasn't excited to go after booking hotels and finding childcare. But she explained her feelings, that she wasn't ready to be away from the baby, and I realized I was being a bit selfish. I should have talked with her first, instead of trying to surprise her with an impromptu vacation.

Small gestures are a much better and more manageable way to show affection for your partner. An "I love you text" when you are apart, a kiss at the start of the day, a home-cooked meal or their favorite takeout. It may not sound sexy, but getting someone food from their favorite Chinese restaurant can be the most romantic thing in the world.

Schedule Intimate Time

What's sexier than breaking out a calendar and saying, "hey, when are you free?" Okay, that doesn't actually sound sexy at all. But with the cramped work schedule, taking care of the baby, and everything else in your lives, scheduling intimacy may be the best solution to a temporary dry spell. Pick a time once a week when you and your partner can have a night to yourselves (after the baby has gone to bed.)

Put the phones away, unplug the television, and spend some time talking, cuddling, and hopefully more. Remind your partner why you find them attractive, and don't be afraid to make the first move. Your significant other is likely just as sexually frustrated as you are. That being said, if they aren't in the mood, there are other ways to be intimate. Simply holding one another, kissing, and talking about anything but the baby can help strengthen your connection.

Get Naked and Give Gifts

It can be hard to remember that you and your partner are sexual creatures when you are constantly clothed in the classic parent's uniform: baggy t-shirt, flat grey sweatpants, and well-worn slippers. Shed those clothes whenever you can, even if you don't plan to have sex. Feeling comfortable with your body and even doing something as simple as walking around naked can ease the stress; not only that, but it's more than likely to lead to something more.

You can also spark intimacy with some sexually suggestive gifts. If you've been with your significant other for a long time, your sex life may have become a bit stagnant. This can aggravate the intimacy struggle that follows birth; the solution is to try new things. Talk with your partner about their fantasies, and surprise them with a gift that fulfills them.

Reclaim Some Space

A baby can sometimes feel like a very territorial and poorly behaved roommate. Suddenly, this tiny tyrant has taken over the whole of your house. They are up late, making noise and constantly present when you are trying to spend time with your partner. Pictures of the baby replace photos of your time together as a couple, everyone asks about your child whenever they see you, and every single event seems to revolve around your infant. It's hard to feel attractive when you've lost your identity as an individual and as a couple. The solution is to reclaim a bit of space!

Now, this doesn't mean deprioritizing your baby. But there are little things you can do to remind your partner and yourself that you are people. Keep some photos of your time as a couple, talk to your partner about fun trips you took before the baby, and try to have a space in the house that is just for you and your significant other. Recapture some ground for yourselves, and you'll be surprised at how quickly the intimacy returns.

Your Baby, Your Relationship, and Your Work Life: How Can You Balance Everything?

Now that we've talked about a few ways to reignite the intimacy in your relationship, let's move to the juggling act of fatherhood. You need to be a parent and a partner, and you'll also likely need to keep working. Keeping all these plates spinning isn't easy but keeping your finances in order is an absolute necessity. In our next chapter, we'll discuss a few ways to keep your work and life balanced, manage your finances, analyze expenses, and save money during the first year of your baby's life.

Dad Hacks From Chapter 7

Relationship Hack #1: You'll Need to Sacrifice a Few Things. Parenthood is all about sacrifice, and you'll have to become comfortable letting certain things go. Your life has changed dramatically, and you'll lose some of your autonomy. Some of it will come back in time, but some won't (and that's okay!)

Relationship Hack #2: Prepare for Sleeplessness. Sleep is incredibly important, but getting the right amount of rest as a new parent is not possible. Watch for the signs of sleep exhaustion, including confusion, lack of energy, and irritability. Do what you can to nap when your partner is watching the baby, and know that your sleep schedule will eventually normalize.

Relationship Hack #3: Watch for the Signs of Postpartum Depression. PPD is incredibly serious, so watch for the signs that your partner may suffer from this illness. These signs include:

- Lack of motivation
- Mood swings
- Avoidance of others
- Thoughts of suicide or harming the baby

If you recognize the symptoms of PPD, contact your doctor immediately.

Relationship Hack #4: Be Patient With Your Partner. Being a new parent is incredibly difficult, and it's understandable to get frustrated when your significant other makes a mistake. Try to see the situation from their shoes and understand you are both tired and stressed out. Patience pays off, and when you give your spouse the benefit of the doubt, they are more likely to return the favor.

Relationship Hack #5: Rekindle Your Sex Life. Don't let the intimacy in your relationship slip away due to the responsibilities of parenthood. Remind your partner that you find them sexually desirable, find time to spend together, and respark the fire of love in your life. It may take a few weeks or months after the baby is born, but once your partner is ready, get back in the bedroom!

Chapter 8

How to Juggle Work and Life as a New Dad

A father isn't just a caretaker and provider, he is also a performer. Like someone spinning plates or juggling flaming bowling pins, a dad needs to understand how to keep everything moving together in (almost) perfect harmony. Once your child is born, you can basically bisect your life into two major parts: time spent at work and time spent at home. Both carry a significant amount of importance: your time at home life will define how much of your energy you can dedicate to being a father and partner, while your time spent at work will determine how well you can provide for your family. Achieving a perfect balance between these two parts isn't possible, but you'll want to get as close as you can. Let's look at a few ways you can balance work and life as a new dad.

5 Ways to Balance Work and Life as a New Dad

1. Set Your Priorities

While arranging your time in both your role as a dad and a worker won't be simple, the process will be easier if you set short and long term priorities. Obviously, you want to spend as much time as possible with your child. At the same time, you need to make sure that your family is supported financially. This will require a bit of compromise in each of your roles.

You'll need to be realistic about what you can accomplish in a day and plan accordingly. If your job frequently requires you to stay late, it may not be possible to agree to extra responsibilities for your child. This is an example from a bit later on in my parenthood journey, I was asked to coach my first child's soccer team. Unfortunately, due to my work duties I had to decline. Instead, I made sure to take time off or leave early on days when there were games and attend as many as possible. Making a compromise like this can show your child you care about them without causing you to lose too much ground at work.

2. Use Your Time as Effectively as Possible

Try to plan out the hours of your day and set aside as much time as possible for your child. This could mean waking up a bit earlier to spend time with the baby before you leave for work or sacrificing drinks with your co-workers to come home and play with your child before bed. You can still have a bit of time to yourself and your friends, but remember tip #1: you have to decide what your priorities are and dedicate the majority of your time to those.

You can also plan ahead and change your behavior to save time with activities like meal prep. Choose a day of the week, like Sunday, and make all of your lunches for the week. This will give you a bigger chunk of time each day to either catch up on work or play with your child. There are also apps and services that can be great time savers. Grocery delivery services can save you hours of wandering through stores, a task that can be all the more difficult with an infant. I can't tell you how many times I've been stuck on a work call with my child in the cart, desperately trying to navigate my conversation while preventing my kid from grabbing food from the shelves. In my experience, it's better to pay a bit more to have the whole shopping ordeal taken care of for you.

3. Discuss Issues with Your Partner

Remember, you aren't in this alone! Talk to your significant other about your work-life concerns, and see what solutions they may have. They will most likely be willing to take on more baby tasks on certain days to ease your stress. For instance, if you have a big meeting coming up the next day, ask your partner if they would be willing to watch the baby so you can prepare. You may feel guilty asking them to do extra work, but if something is important, I'm sure your partner will be understanding.

You can also make plans with your significant other concerning both of your work schedules. With my partner, we had an issue early on balancing child-care and both of our jobs. We were trying to save a bit of money by not using a daycare every day of the work week, but the stress was starting to get overwhelming. We decided it was well worth the extra money, and sacrificed some money we had been saving for a vacation. Even though it was sad to see our Jamaican cruise money go up in smoke, it was a necessary compromise to help that work-life balance become more manageable.

4. Turn off the Tech

Both my partner and I have our own separate technology addictions, each for different reasons. She is a true crime fanatic and constantly listening to podcasts or perusing forums, while I'm always plugged into my fantasy football league. After the baby, we both had to take a step back and realize we were hooked up to our devices for a majority of the day.

Part of the issue with completely cutting myself off from my phone and computer is that sometimes my work needs to contact me after hours. Admittedly, I made myself a bit too available to calls and emails; a lot of the time, it was something that could have easily waited until work hours. So after the baby was born, I let my department know: unless it was of vital importance, I wouldn't be answering messages outside of the office. Surprisingly, they had no problem with this at all! This gave me much more time to spend with my child, and helped me establish boundaries between my work life and my home life.

5. Talk with Your Work about Flexibility

Speaking of work discussions, you will likely have told your supervisors about the baby well before they are born. Part of this discussion should be about your work hours, and trying to create a schedule that allows you to help out at home as much as possible. You'd be surprised how many workplaces will be flexible when it comes to childcare, and there may even be programs your company has set up to assist you.

Working from home is one way to help you save time, and if your job is the type that can be done remotely, talk to your boss about splitting your hours between the office and your home. By working remotely, you can eliminate the time wasted commuting, as well as take small breaks throughout the day to spend time with your child. Working from home can also reduce the financial burden of finding childcare services. Overall, remote work is one of the best ways to get the balance you are looking for when it comes to your job and home life.

Financial Tips for New Dads: How to Get More Out of Your Money

Part of the reason that creating a work-life balance is so difficult is that, no matter how you slice it, having a kid requires a significant amount of money. You want to spend every second with your baby, but at the same time, you have to shoulder the financial burden of food, diapers, toys, and everything else that your child needs. To make this easier, you'll want to make sure your finances are as orderly as possible. Here are a few tips that can make that process much smoother.

Tip #1: Create a Budget

The first step to improving your financial health is to create a budget. Map out your income and expenses, taking special note of whether you are spending your money on "wants" or "needs". When I first put together a budget, I noticed I was spending an *insane* amount of money on coffee each month. I didn't think much of it as I was calculating the amount, saying to myself "plenty of people get a coffee every day, how much could it really be?" After I hit enter on the calculator, I was shocked to see I was spending **over \$200** on coffee each and every month. After raising my hands to the sky and cursing my favorite coffee shop, I purchased a nice coffee maker online. Now getting coffee is a very rare treat, and I have more money for the things that matter.

Tip #2: Take Advantage of Credit Card Benefits

Building credit and using all of the benefits your bank offers is essential to strengthening your finances. If your credit score is low, fixing it should be a priority. Make a list of all of your payments, whether it be for your car, cards, or any loans you have, and ensure you consistently pay them on time. Credit utilization is especially important; if your cards are constantly maxed out, your credit score will drop dramatically. Over time your score will rise, making it easier to get loan approval and lower interest.

You should also look at your credit card benefits. Many cards have cash back or redeemable points that come with making purchases. These points can be used for rewards like food, gas, airline miles, and many other things that can help reduce your expenses. As long as you can pay the cards off, try to put as much of your purchasing as possible onto your credit cards (using your debit card likely won't give you the same benefits as using your credit cards.)

Tip #3: Make Sure You Have an Emergency Fund

Life is unpredictable, and having an emergency fund can give you one of the most valuable things a parent can have: peace of mind. Shortly after our first child was born, I got into a car accident. Thankfully I was the only one in the car, and I wasn't hurt. I wish I could say the same for my Honda! With my vehicle totaled, and my insurance slow to approve my claim, I had to pay for the damages myself so I could keep commuting to work. Luckily, I had my emergency fund; what could have been an incredibly difficult problem was downgraded to only a minor inconvenience.

For your emergency fund to have a sufficient amount of money, make sure it can cover 6 to 12 months of your monthly expenses. This money can come in handy for a number of situations including:

- Vehicle Troubles
- Job Loss
- Medical Emergency
- Unexpected Travel Expenses
- Emergency Home Repairs

Tip #4: Get Life Insurance and Make a Will

It's tough to think about, but one important financial factor is preparing for the worst case scenario. An official will and solid life insurance policy can be massively helpful to your family in the event of your death, helping both your partner and your child through what would already be an overwhelming period of time. If you can try, try to get your life insurance through your employers, as they usually offer the best rates. Shoot for a policy that covers 10 times your annual income, as this would give your family a substantial buffer if you were to suddenly pass away.

As for a will, this will be something you'll want to talk about with your partner. It can be tempting to avoid this as long as possible, as the thought of you or your significant other passing away is devastating. But for legal reasons, neglecting to have a will can make the already arduous process of spousal death that much more complicated. Talk to an estate lawyer in your area about what the best way to draw up a will, as well as decide who will have the power of attorney for both your finances and healthcare. I chose my partner, but it's entirely possible you have someone else in mind. This person will be able to control both your money and your medical care if you are ever unable to do so, like if you are in a coma or any other type of incapacitated state.

Tip #5: Choose Safe Investments

While keeping your money in a savings account may seem safe, it won't do much in the way of growth. Check what retirement contribution plans your employer offers, like a 401k. You'll also want to see what wealth management services your bank offers, as well as plans you can create to start saving for your child's college education. A 529 plan is a good example of this type of savings; with a 529 plan, you can deposit money without paying federal taxes and won't pay penalties when funds are withdrawn for educational purposes. Anyone can contribute to a 529, meaning that relatives and loved ones can put money in as a gift to you or your children.

You'll also want to avoid risky or highly speculative forms of investing, like cryptocurrency or individual stocks. Total market ETFs are okay, but the issue comes in when you place large amounts of money into what is essentially gambling. I remember getting a hot tip from a friend about this smaller cryptocurrency, and regrettably threw a few thousand dollars down. I thought "well if he's right, and this goes up 1000%, my child's education will be fully paid for! I'd be irresponsible not to do it, right?" You can guess how this story ends; let's just say, I'm still saving for future education expenses. Skip the risky bets, and stick to sustainable growth over the long term.

Tip #6: Don't Forget to Have a "Fun" Fund!

Just because you aren't blowing all your paychecks on extravagant getaways or expensive toys doesn't mean you can't have fun every now and then. In the early days after the baby is born, when the stress is building, get together with your partner and talk about a fun future trip. Brainstorm up places you've always wanted to go, look up flight and hotel packages, talk about all the different activities you want to do while you're there, and put the plan down on paper. Obviously this won't take place further down the road, but you can even talk about whether you'd be comfortable having close relatives watch the baby for the duration of the trip. This can be incredibly helpful to alleviate that "cooped up" feeling that often accompanies early parenthood.

Once the plan is set, start saving. During those planning stages make sure to draft up the rough costs this type of trip would incur, including travel expenses, food, lodging, and childcare if that applies. You can create a savings account specifically for the trip (labeling it something like "Las Vegas 2025" or whatever name would apply) and make regular deposits. This also gives you and your partner something to look forward to, and a discussion topic that does not involve your child.

How Can I Save Money on My Baby's Necessities?

Having a baby is expensive, and feeling that financial strain can make an already stressful situation that much worse. Here are a few ways you can save money during the first year of your baby's life.

- *Feeding:* If possible, talk to your partner about primarily breastfeeding as opposed to formula feeding, as this can drastically reduce food costs. Look into purchasing a decent breast pump along with breast milk storage bottles and bags. This is what we did with our second child, and by the end of the first year we had saved almost $1000.
- *Diapers:* I'm personally guilty of using disposable diapers, so I completely understand not having the time or energy to go the more affordable route. But if you can, cloth diapers are far easier on the wallet and way better for the environment. Cloth diapers are reusable, and there are even services that will deliver them to your home and give you better prices if you buy in bulk.
- *Baby Toys:* As parents, we all want to spoil our children with all the toys they could want. The fact of the matter is, infants really don't need much in that first year. Stick with a few baby-safe toys, mostly ones that they can chew on without any risk of choking. Your baby isn't going to get bored of one toy and want another, because frankly, they aren't forming those types of memories yet.
- *Baby Clothes:* Baby's grow quickly, and while it may look cute to have them decked out in neat outfits for every stage of their growth, it just isn't financially sound. Talk to your friends who have also had children, as they may have some

secondhand baby clothes you can use. If you do buy clothes, try to shop for the deals and see what you can get for more affordable prices. That big price tag onesie may look cute on the rack, but once it's covered in stains, you'll probably regret the money you spent.

Baby Care Tasks Worksheet

To help you and your partner allocate your time more efficiently, try to track how many hours you spend completing various household and childcare related tasks each week. I've placed a sample chart below. You may want to modify the chart with your own tasks, but this is a good framework to help you get started.

Task	Monday	Tuesday	Wednesday	Thursday	Friday	Saturday	Sunday
Baby Bath Time							
Baby Play Time							
Laundry							
Getting Baby Ready for Sleep							
Cooking							
Washing Dishes							
Paying Bills							
Vehicle Maintenance							
Shopping for Food							
Taking Care of Pets							
Mowing/Gardening							
Going to Work							
Cleaning the House							
Taking the Baby Outdoors							
School work (if applicable)							
Talking on the Phone (for work or other purposes)							
Changing Diapers							
Cleaning Up Baby-Related Messes							

Babies May Take a Lot of Time and Money, But It's Always Worth It

Balancing both your time and finances may be difficult, but once you find that sweet spot, you'll start to notice everything gets a bit easier. Believe me, it's possible to succeed at work AND make sure your baby feels loved, but it may take a bit for you to master your juggling act. Now, we've covered a lot of topics in this book, and it's understandable if there are certain sections you want to review. In the conclusion that follows, we'll look back at the subjects we've talked about and give a brief overview for each.

Dad Hacks From Chapter 8

Balance Hack #1: Prioritize What's Important. It's a tough pill to swallow, but the fact is there just isn't time for everything. Make a list of all of your responsibilities, and try to rank them based on importance. Being a dad will come first most of the time, this is a give-in; that being said, maintaining your status at work is also vital to your family's financial health. Learn to prioritize the most essential activities, and become comfortable with compromise.

Balance Hack #2: Time Management is Essential. There are only so many hours in the day, but you'd be surprised how much time we waste. Between our phones, TV, drinks after work, and every other leisurely activity, we rarely use each day to its full potential. Breakdown how you use your time, eliminating unavoidable activities like work at sleep. Look at the hours you have left and try to fill them with as much productivity as possible (making sure to give yourself a small chunk each day for "me-time").

Balance Hack #3: Prepare for the Unexpected. Parenthood is a lot like improve, and you'll need to roll with the punches when it comes to dealing with the challenges that get thrown your way. Part of this is thinking about the more unfortunate turns life can take, like…well, death. Creating a will and getting a life insurance policy, while a bit of a bummer, can give you valuable peace of mind as you raise your children. Knowing your significant other and children will be safe in the case of your passing can allow you to focus on the present, and be the best dad you possibly can.

Balance Hack #4: Create a Budget. Budgeting is a life skill that can help anyone, parent or not. Calculating your income and tallying up your expenses can help you keep a healthy financial flow, as well as highlight any extraneous spending you may have. I was shocked when I laid out my budget on how much I was spending on things like eating out at restaurants and getting coffee every day. Cooking at home and making my own coffee saved me hundreds of dollars every month, which allowed me to make more significant contributions to my child's college fund.

Balance Hack #5: Don't Forget the Fun. While it is important to work hard and give your all when it comes to being a father, you still need to schedule in some time for yourself. Neglecting to do so can lead to increased stress, which will start to hamper your performance both in the workplace and at home. Make sure to invest time in a hobby, and try your best to have a night out with friends every once and a while. Your spouse will also need some "me" time, so talk with each other about how you can adjust your schedules to make this happen.

Conclusion

Despite the trials and tribulations of parenthood, nothing can bring you more joy in this life than having a baby. Yes, it comes with responsibilities, but you'll be amazed what you can accomplish when you have the love of a family behind you. No one is a perfect dad, even those of us that have been fathers for many years. But with genuine care, attention, and a willingness to stick out even the toughest monuments, you can give your child the foundation they need to grow up happy, confident, and ready for life's challenges. Remember, many things in life are challenging in the beginning; few things worth fighting for are easy. But just like gold hidden deep beneath the earth, your baby is a treasure. The first 12 months can be tough, but with the information I've compiled here, and your own strong will, I know you will be able to get through it.

To help you review the information we've covered in this book, let's go chapter by chapter and highlight the most important bits of information.

Chapter 1: What to Expect and What to Do When Your Baby is Born

In Chapter 1 we discussed how to prep your home for the baby's arrival and what you can expect in the first 24 hours after you return from the hospital. This included ways to babyproof your home, like taking care of any sharp corners, dangerous cords, or potentially consumable chemicals. For the first 24 hours, we looked at what should be done at the hospital (like expecting the placenta and helping your spouse get skin-to-skin contact with the baby) along with the first feedings and all tests that will take place right after birth.

Chapter 2: Basic Care for Your Baby

Chapter 2 covered the basic ways to take care of your baby, including:

- *Changing Diapers:* As a dad, you'll be changing your fair share of diapers, so it's best to be prepared. The chapter talks about how to pack and bring a diaper bag, the proper way to change a diaper, and all the associated materials you'll need to do a diaper change.
- *Bathing the Baby:* We also discussed the right way to bathe a baby and how frequently your baby needs a bath. The chapter also covers how full a bath should be, what temperature the water should reach, and what types of soaps to use when washing your baby.
- *How to Deal With Crying:* Chapter 2 talks about the reasons that babies cry, and when crying is normal or due to an illness (like colic). We also discussed the danger of shaken baby syndrome, and the proper ways to help your child when they are crying.

The chapter concluded by discussing SIDS, including the causes, risk factors, and how to prevent this syndrome from occurring.

Chapter 3: How to Feed Your Baby the Right Way

In Chapter 3 we covered the right ways to feed your baby, including how to establish a feeding schedule. Your baby may be getting its nutrients from a few sources, including breastfeeding or bottle feeding with formula. The chapter then goes into introducing solids at around the four month mark and how to properly store these foods. The chapter closes on keeping your baby hydrated, talking about when it's okay to give your baby water and when they can have other beverages like juice.

Chapter 4: How to Help Your Baby Sleep

Chapter 4 was all about making sure your baby gets the right amount of sleep to facilitate healthy brain development and avoid cognition issues later in life. The chapter begins by discussing infant sleeping patterns in different stages, including:

- 0-3 months
- 3-6 months
- 6-12 months

We also covered the signs that your baby isn't getting enough sleep, including that they are having trouble getting settled, rubbing their eyes, fussing, and moving around uneasily. We also talked about some healthy sleep tips, like making sure your baby gets natural sunlight in the morning, establishing a bedtime routine, and the best way to rock your baby to sleep. The chapter closes on some common sleep problems you'll encounter during the first 12 months of your baby's life and how you can solve them.

Chapter 5: How to Teach Your Baby to Develop Self-Regulation

In Chapter 5 we went over the temperament of infants, and how learning self-control and self-regulation early on can help your baby as they develop into their adolescence. To avoid undue stress, a baby needs to learn to self-soothe, but the skill will grow slowly. The chapter covers the self-regulation abilities of infants over the first 12 months of their lives, primarily in months 0-3, 3-6, and 6-12. Each section covers the different behaviour's your baby will exhibit, and some tips on how you can help create the right environment for them to self-soothe. The chapter closes on some ways you can increase self-control and self-confidence in your child, as well as the best ways to tune-in to their temperament.

Chapter 6: How to Help Your Baby Develop Their Emotional and Mental Health

Following the chapter on self-regulation, we covered the further development of your baby's mental and emotional health. Chapter 6 starts on some tips for each developmental stage, including:

- *Month 0-3:* Engaging their senses, using baby talk, soothing, and stimulating
- *Month 3-6:* Showing your baby photos, mirroring their sounds, and encouraging them to interact with objects
- *Month 6-12:* Allowing your baby to explore the house, speaking full words to them, and connecting sounds with gestures

The chapter then went on to talk about ways to bond with your baby. These tips include smiling/talking with your baby, making funny faces, singing, getting skin-to-skin contact, and having one-on-one time. The chapter ends on a breakdown of each stage and the best ways to bond with your baby during each.

Chapter 7: How to Keep Your Relationship Going Strong, Even After Having a Baby

In Chapter 7 we talked about how having a baby can affect your relationships, and the different issues that can cause strife right after the birth of your child. Some of these issues included:

- Needing to restructure your lives
- Lack of sleep and the associated problems that creates
- The feelings of frustration or hopelessness of early parenthood
- Focusing all of your attention on your baby and none on your partner
- The strain a baby can put on communication
- The lack of spontaneity once you have a child
- The possibility of postpartum depression
- The lack of sex during the first year of parenthood

The chapter then covered five tips to helping your relationship say strong post baby:

1. See Things from Your Partner's Perspective
2. Schedule a Weekly Check-in
3. Avoid Criticism and Talk Efficiently
4. Make Time For Each other
5. "Parent" Each Other

The chapter closed on some ways to rekindle your sex life after childbirth, like creating passion, making small gestures, scheduling intimate time, getting naked, and reclaiming some space for you and your significant other.

Chapter 8: How to Juggle Work and Life as a New Dad

The final chapter covered ways to balance your work life and home life as a new father. Chapter 8 begins with five balancing tips, including:

1. Set Your Priorities
2. Use Your Time as Effectively as Possible
3. Discuss Issues with Your Partner
4. Turn off the Tech (take a break from devices)

5. Talk with Your Work about Flexibility

The chapter then delved into some financial tips for new dads and how to get more out of your money. These tips included:

1. Create a Budget
2. Take Advantage of Credit Card Benefits
3. Create an Emergency Fund
4. Get Life Insurance and Make a Will
5. Make Sure You Choose Safe Investments
6. Create a "Fun" Fund (for vacations, etc)

The chapter closes on how to save money on baby necessities, like food, diapers, toys, and clothes. I also included a baby care tasks worksheet, so you and your partner can see if you are splitting house and baby chores evenly.

What I Want You To Take Away

Every father starts as a novice, and with this book, I hope to impart as much knowledge as possible to make the journey a bit easier. By paying attention to the little things, strengthening your partnership with your spouse, and remembering to tend to your baby's emotional needs, you can set your family up for a bright and prosperous future.

If you enjoyed this book, it would mean the world to me if you left a review on Amazon. I believe the work I've put into these chapters can help new fathers reduce some of the stress of early parenthood and learn some tips that can make the first 12 months a more manageable mountain to summit. While the first year may seem arduous, I promise you will look back one day and miss when your child was this small. Take pictures, videos, make scrapbooks, do anything you can to crystallize these memories for the future. That's one of the most important tips I can give you: cherish every moment.

Life is short, and your children will only be babies once. Yes, it will get tough. But I promise you, every sleepless night, every argument with your partner, every dirty diaper, is 100% worth it in the end.

I would be glad to hear your feedback about this book, both from the perspective of how it applied to your experience and what you learned from your real-life experience that could have been included here. Feel free to email me at: http://williamhardingauthor.com/.

If you think the book was helpful and that it is worthy of a nice review, please leave one on Amazon or your venue of choice. This will help dads that you don't even know to prepare for this phase of their life and look forward to enjoying their future.

Thanks for reading this work. I look forward to creating more in the future.

Reviews

As an independent author with a small marketing budget, reviews are my livelihood on this platform. If you enjoyed this book, I'd really appreciate it if you left your honest feedback. I love hearing from my readers, and I personally read every single review.

Join the Dads Club Community

DAD's Club: Support Group For Dads | Facebook

References

Printed in the USA
CPSIA information can be obtained
at www.ICGtesting.com
LVHW012217181223
766859LV00012B/701